HOW TO CHOOSE

YOUR BEST

BUSINESS

ENTITY

For

REAL ESTATE

INVESTING

LLC, S CORP, C CORP, PARTNERSHIP, OR DBA?

MICHAEL LANTRIP

Attorney | Accountant | Investor

THE AUTHOR

Michael Lantrip has written and published three #1 Best Selling Amazon books.

"How To Do A Section 1031 Like Kind Exchange"

All of the top Real Estate Investors use Section 1031 instead of paying taxes on Capital Gains and Depreciation Recapture. Then they use IRS money to buy more property.

"50 Real Estate Investing Calculations"

When Real Estate Investors say, "I wish I'd known that," this is what they are talking about. Real Estate Investing Calculations are the Rules of Real Estate Investing, and you won't be successful without knowing them. A basic rule of Business Management is "In order to manage, you must first measure." And that's the purpose of Real Estate Investing Calculations.

"Tax Cuts And Jobs Act For Real Estate Investors: The New Rules"

<u>Real Estate is poised for the largest growth cycle in 30 years after passage of the Tax Cuts And Jobs Act. And the big winners will be the first Real Estate Investors to learn The New Rules.</u>

Michael Lantrip, Attorney at Law, is licensed to practice law in Texas, North Carolina, Virginia, and the District of Columbia.

He has a B.B.A. in Finance from the University of Houston School of Business, and he has a Juris Doctor (J.D.) in Law from the University of Texas School of Law.

He is admitted to practice in all Courts in Texas, North Carolina, Virginia, and the District of Columbia, as well as the U.S. Tax Court, U.S. Federal District Court, Eastern District of Texas, and the D.C. Court of Appeals.

He practices in the fields of Tax Law, Real Estate Law, Corporate and Business Law, and Wills, Trusts and Estates.

As a Criminal Defense Attorney, he has taken three cases to the Texas Court of Criminal Appeals, winning two of them.

As a County Attorney, he handled almost 2,000 misdemeanor criminal cases.

Formerly a Tax Examiner for the IRS, and a Tax Accountant for a Big 8 Accounting Firm, he has also been a Newspaper Reporter, Radio Announcer, Radio News Director, Television Reporter and Anchorman, Television Executive News Producer, and Military Intelligence Analyst.

In addition to 35 years of practicing law, he built one of the first computerized Abstract Plants and operated his own Title Insurance Company, and has been an Approved Title Attorney for seven national Title Insurance Underwriters.

He has handled over 2,000 real estate closings.

Prior to his law career, he was a Radio Announcer at WQTE in Detroit during the "Motown" era, and he was a DJ at KIKK in Houston when it was named "Country Music Station of the Year" by Billboard Magazine.

He has written and produced more than 1,000 half-hour Television Newscasts.

He has written over 700 stories as a daily Newspaper Reporter.

He has logged over 8,000 hours on the radio.

He is a Lifetime Member of Mensa.

As a Real Estate Investor, his activities have ranged from Travel Trailers to Office Buildings, and from on-campus Condos to hundreds of acres of raw land.

His Amazon Author Page is:

amazon.com/Michael-Lantrip/e/B01N2ZRGUY

His personal website is MichaelLantrip.com.

He was named a Top Writer 2018 by Quora.com.

FOREWORD

Welcome to the world of Real Estate Investing.

It is different from any other type of investing.

You can create lifetime wealth in the millions of dollars, starting with modest, safe investments, using:

◊   Financial leverage,

◊ Compounding,

◊ Asset appreciation,

◊ Special tax treatment, and

◊ The time value of money.

And the two most important decisions that you will make are:

1.) The type of Business Entity that is best for you, and

2.) How you want to be taxed by the IRS.

Get them wrong, and you will crash and burn.

But, get them right, and you will enjoy all of the success you could ever imagine.

And, "one size" definitely does not "fit all."

Exactly the opposite!

Don't listen to anyone who says that you should "use this entity for this activity, and that one for the other activity."

This is custom work.

No one knows which Entity you should use, or how you should elect to be taxed, except you, and you don't even know until you've finished this book, and realize what all of the variables are.

You have 6 choices.

1.) Sole Proprietorship.

2.) Limited Liability Company.

3.) C Corporation.

4.) Subchapter S Corporation.

5.) General Partnership.

6.) Limited Partnership.

You will be using one or more of these Entities.

In most situations, you will also be allowed to elect how you want to be taxed.

And only <u>you</u> can make the decision, so get ready.

This is the most comprehensive book available on the subject of Real Estate Investing, and the first one written in an organized format and in Plain English.

I will provide the information and explanations that you need, but you will make the decision.

This is your first step in what I believe will be the most enjoyable, and important, journey you will ever make.

Welcome.

COPYRIGHT PAGE

MICHAEL LANTRIP

The Author has taken reasonable precautions in the preparation of this book and believes that the information presented in the book is accurate as of the date of publication. However, neither the Author nor the Publisher assumes any responsibility for any errors or omissions. The Author and the Publisher specifically disclaim any liability resulting from the use or application of the information contained in this book, and the information is not intended to serve as legal, tax, or other financial advice related to individual situations.

DISCLAIMER

Although I am a lawyer, I am not your lawyer. I would be honored if I were, but I am not.

Reading this book does not create an attorney-client relationship between us. This book should not be used as a substitute for the advice of a competent attorney admitted or authorized to practice law in your jurisdiction.

CONTENTS

INTRODUCTION

For the first time, all in one book, you have every possible way that you can operate your business and pay your taxes, and the advantages and disadvantages of each.

Your success, or failure, in Real Estate Investing will be determined (of course) by the decisions you make along the way.

But the **two most important decisions you will ever make** are:

1.) The type of Business that is best for you, and

2.) How you want to be taxed by the IRS.

In other words, which type of business formation will serve you best?

As of January 1, 2018, the Tax Cuts And Jobs Act (TCJA) has totally changed your previous "Choice of Entity" decision, primarily because of the way in which taxes are assessed. And you get to choose how you want to be taxed.

So, this is a perfect time for you to look at the question of your Best Business Entity, and do the analysis and decision-making that will give you the best chance of success for the coming years.

This book will guide you through the process.

You have 6 choices.

1. Sole Proprietorship.

2. Limited Liability Company.

3. C Corporation.

4. Subchapter S Corporation.

5. General Partnership.

6. Limited Partnership.

I will explain how each Entity works, how it is formed, how it is financed, and how it is taxed.

Then I will explain the Management of each one, including

◊ Operating the business,

◊ Buying real estate,

◊ Contributing owned real estate,

◊ Selling real estate,

◊ Providing personal services, and

◊ Bookkeeping.

And for each Entity, I will explain the Liability involved, for both the Entity itself and the Individual who formed it.

I will also explain the Taxation, Federal and State, for both the Individual and for the Entity.

The Table of Contents contains the page numbers of each explanation, so you can switch back and forth between Chapters for a better understanding.

And as a bonus, I will provide a warning against a couple of entities that you should never consider, under any circumstances, and I will explain why.

This book will serve as your Authority on the entire subject of Best Business Entity, and it will also serve as a Reference Book when you need to know the answer to a specific question.

You might be ready to dive into the analysis right now; if so you can just start with Chapter 1.

But, as I indicated, there have been a lot of changes in the tax law and business law recently, and you might want to refresh your understanding by looking at Chapters 9 through 16. The explanations are in Plain English.

These Chapters cover the six critical elements of Real Estate Investing that were changed on January 1, 2018 when the new tax law, the Tax Cuts And Jobs Act (TCJA), went into effect.

These changes are the biggest in Real Estate Investing for the past 30 years.

They are:

1.) Individual Tax Rates.

2.) Corporate Tax Rates.

3.) Capital Gains.

4.) Bonus Depreciation.

5.) Pass-Through Entities.

6.) Qualified Business Income.

If you are current on all of this information and ready to start right in with Chapter 1, you can do that, and then refer to the later Chapters when you need to.

I hope that this book will help you to create the foundation for your success in Real Estate Investing.

Welcome.

CHAPTER 1

SOLE PROPRIETORSHIP

OVERVIEW

Some people say that a Sole Proprietorship is not a Business Entity.

It is.

It is <u>not</u> a Legal Entity, but it <u>is</u> a Business Entity.

It is a form of doing business, just like all of the other Business Entities.

A Sole Proprietorship is simply you, owning (and usually operating) a business.

It is the simplest form of doing business.

That's why this first Chapter will be shorter than the others.

Here's how the Sole Proprietorship works.

Let's say that you want to start a business as a Bookkeeper.

You buy a computer, software, phone, all-in-one printer, desk, chair, filing cabinet, bookcases, and miscellaneous office supplies.

You choose a name, build a website, set aside a room in your home for an office, and decide on some form of advertising.

Then you wait.

You are a Sole Proprietor.

It is just you, operating a business, and that business is a Sole Proprietorship.

There are various forms of this arrangement, and I could make this more complicated, but it really isn't.

For a Real Estate Investor, if you choose to buy your first real estate investment in your own name, this also meets the definition of Sole Proprietorship, and you are operating a business, even though it is a rental real estate business, with only one investment property.

And you will probably be buying much of the same equipment as the Bookkeeper, because you are also now running a business in addition to being a Real Estate Investor.

FORMATION

There is no "formation" for a Sole Proprietorship.

There are no legal requirements for creating the business.

But there are other steps that you might have to take at the same time that you start to operate the business.

For instance, you might also be required to obtain a license, such as a firearms license, or a certification of some type, or register with some agency.

Or you might not.

It depends on the laws in your State.

Being a Real Estate Investor does not require a license or registration.

You don't even have to operate with a business name.

To use our Example, if you are a Bookkeeper, and all of your customers knew that you are, and they just came to you for their bookkeeping services, then you might just operate as John Doe, Bookkeeper.

But if you decide to use a business name, you will probably be required to file an Assumed Name Certificate for the name of the business in the County Records, and possibly with the Secretary of State, so that everyone will be able to see who they are doing business with, and where you are located.

You can just pick a name that is not being used in the area, such as Premier Bookkeeping Services, and use it.

Remember that when you are signing your name on certain documents related to the business, you should use "John Doe, DBA Premier Bookkeeping Services." The "DBA" stands for "doing business as." Signing in this way stipulates the capacity in which you are acting. It does not relieve you of any liability, but establishes that you are acting in a business capacity, not a personal capacity. It could make a difference if there is a problem.

The Assumed Name is still not a legal entity, separate from the Sole Proprietor.

Also, there might be some required compliance with zoning restrictions, but it is not usually anything more than adhering to "commercial" or "business" zones, and avoiding "residential" zones. But with the large number of people using home offices today, those rules are probably not being enforced.

It would be unusual if you were prohibited from operating your Real Estate Investing business from your home.

Of course, if you were doing a lot of construction, and you were storing material and equipment in your driveway and yard, there could be a problem.

You will need to obtain an FEIN – Federal Employer Identification Number, also called an EIN, even if you have no employees. More on that below.

But there are no formal steps required to "form" a Sole Proprietorship.

You just do it.

FINANCING

A Sole Proprietorship is normally created when you purchase the necessary equipment for the business, using your personal funds.

So there is no "financing" involved, in terms of borrowing money and incurring debt.

If you <u>do</u> go to a lender to obtain funds, the type of loan that you would be offered would be a personal loan, secured with personal assets and personal credit. The assets of your business will not normally be used as the only security for the loan.

However, you should keep track of all of your purchases of business assets and supplies in meticulous detail, and list all of your personal property that you will use in the business. I discuss this in more detail in "Bookkeeping" below.

If you choose to buy your first real estate investment in your own name, you will probably get a mortgage for as much of the purchase price as possible, but you will still be required to spend your own money for the down payment.

Again, keep track of your personal expenses, and save all receipts.

And, even though the mortgage is a personal debt and not a business debt, the interest portion of the monthly payments are business expenses, and can be deducted from income.

MANAGEMENT

The management of a Sole Proprietorship is simpler than for any of the Business Entities that I discuss in this book.

That is the main reason that someone would decide to use a Sole Proprietorship form for business.

But there are still rules and conventions that must be followed, as well as rules of the Internal Revenue Code, which all businesses must follow.

OPERATING THE BUSINESS

You just do it the way you want.

As I said, it is the simplest form of business, and there are very few rules.

There are no corporate Officers with specific powers and duties, and you don't have to designate a Manager, or elect a Managing Partner.

It's all up to you.

You must keep track of all of your income, of course.

And you must keep track of all of your expenses.

But documenting everything is the most important thing that you must do.

It is a good idea to set up a separate bank account just for the business, and if that bank account offers a credit card tied to it, it is a good idea to get that as well.

You might want to handle everything with PayPal, and just transfer funds back and forth to and from the bank account.

But, again, receipt everything.

As for having a Budget, you probably don't need one before you start operating, but it is a good idea to write out your plans, informally in your own way, nothing as elaborate as a Business Plan, and include as many numbers as you can come up with for projections of income and expenses.

At some point, when you have some historic data, you should start doing a Budget, with the first one being for six months, just to get into the habit and learn the steps.

After that, you should do a Monthly Income Statement, every month, with an extra column for the income numbers "Year to Date," so that at the end of each month, when you look at what you did the last 30 days, you can also see what you have done so far in the year.

It is the way a professional businessperson runs their business.

Since you will be owning rental real estate, you might want to get a copy of the IRS Publication 527, Residential Rental Property.

You can order a copy, or you can print the pdf at https://www.irs.gov/pub/irs-pdf/p527.pdf. It is 24 pages.

But I warn you, it is confusing.

BUYING REAL ESTATE

As a Sole Proprietor, it will be <u>you</u> who owns the real estate.

A Sole Proprietorship is not a separate legal entity for the purpose of holding property.

You will use your own credit to get the mortgage, which we are assuming you will be getting, and you will use your own funds to make the required down payment, and to pay the transaction costs of acquiring the property.

Actually, this is not much different from operating as a Partnership, S Corp, or LLC in one regard. Even though the Lender would be making the loan to that entity, you will probably be required to sign as a Guarantor. So you are still personally responsible for repayment of the loan.

More on this in the following Chapters.

The real estate will be owned by you, and will become just a business asset, like the filing cabinet.

If you decide to get out of the business of rental real estate, you will not have to dissolve a business and distribute the assets, like you would with a corporation or a partnership. You already own the assets.

You just sell the real estate and pay the Capital Gains and Depreciation Recapture taxes, and you are done.

SELLING REAL ESTATE

If you are in the business of flipping real estate, the real estate that you are selling is considered inventory, the same as if you operate a bicycle store and sell bicycles.

But with the Flipping business, you will be required to use the "accrual" method of accounting instead of the "cash" method. I have devoted an entire Chapter 17 to Flipping Properties.

If you are in the business of owning rental real estate, when you sell one of your rental properties, your net sales proceeds will be treated as Capital Gains.

If you owned the property for one year or less when you sell, the profit will be taxed as Short-Term Capital Gains.

If you owned the property for at least a year and a day when you sell, the profit will be taxed as Long-Term Capital Gains.

PROVIDING SERVICES

If you are a Sole Proprietor, it is presumed that you will be providing the services necessary to operate the business.

You will not receive a paycheck for doing this.

Your compensation for your services will be the profits that the business makes.

Some of the services that your business needs might be provided by an Employee, which you will pay a salary, called W-2 wages, and which I will cover below in "Bookkeeping."

BOOKKEEPING

This is really the crux of managing any business.

You will keep track of all income and expenses of the company.

If you have an employee, you will pay wages, and you will withhold an amount for income taxes, Social Security, and Medicare. You will send that money to the IRS. At the end of the year, you will provide a W-2 to the employee, and send a copy along with other reports to the IRS containing all of the information.

If you pay another person, a non-employee, or company for services, and the total is at least $600 for the tax year, you will send that entity a Form 1099 and send a copy to the IRS.

You will not be able to wait until the end of the year to pay your own income taxes.

You will be required to estimate your tax liability, and send Quarterly Estimates to the IRS. These are funds which the IRS will hold until they receive your Form 1040 which will determine how much income taxes you actually owe. You will claim credit for these Quarterly Estimate deposits against your tax liability.

Unlike wages from a job, rental income is not considered to be earned income.

Also, it is not investment income like capital gains, interest, and dividends.

It is "passive income," and therefore not subject to Self-Employment (SE) Tax of 15.3%, like you must pay on the rest of your earned income.

Also, you will have some assets being used in the business that qualify for depreciation.

This means that you are permitted to deduct, as an expense allowance, a portion of the amount that you paid for the property you purchased to use in the business, and a portion of your own Basis in any property that you already owned and put to use in the business.

There are no State regulations regarding the keeping of books for a Sole Proprietorship, but the IRS expects you to have a responsible set of records available if they should ask to see them. And "responsible" is whatever you think it is, so don't be intimidated.

If you think you would be more comfortable with additional information, the IRS has Publication 583, Starting a Business and Keeping Records.

You can order a copy of the publication from the IRS, or you can print the pdf at https://www.irs.gov/pub/irs-pdf/p583.pdf. It is 27 pages.

You should get a good Tax Preparer to handle the preparation of your tax return and the periodic reports that you must create and send in.

If it is something that you want to do, or enjoy doing, you can do your own Bookkeeping. The rules do not change each year. And doing your own Bookkeeping will make you twice as good at managing your business.

LIABILITY

As I said earlier, the ease of management is the main reason for choosing to operate your business as a Sole Proprietor.

But liability is the main reason for not operating as a Sole Proprietorship.

The Sole Proprietor is responsible for all obligations of the business.

Your personal assets, as well as those used in the business, can be taken to satisfy creditors, claimants, or judgment lien holders.

This means two things.

First, if the business cannot pay its bills, the other assets of the Sole Proprietor can be taken to cover those debts.

Second, if the Sole Proprietor cannot pay his personal debts unrelated to the business, the assets of the business, and the business itself, are subject to being taken to cover those personal debts.

Everything you own is lumped together into one pile.

The Sole Proprietorship and the General Partnership forms of business are the only ones in which there is no protection from personal liability for the owner.

But at least, with the General Partnership, you can be an LLC as a Partner, and create your personal liability protection.

With the Sole Proprietorship, it is just you, responsible for everything.

And don't fall for the claim that you can protect yourself with "an umbrella insurance policy" for a few hundred dollars.

In the first place, the premium is a lot more than that.

Second, the deductible is so high that you could end up with your insurance company reaching a settlement that you will pay most of.

Third, the Exclusions in the policy are usually the exact things that you would be accused of in the lawsuit, so the insurance company can easily, and legally, deny coverage, even if the allegations are false.

Fourth, and finally, an insurance policy is often a magnet for unprincipled individuals and lawyers because they know that there is a certain amount that the insurance company will settle for because the amount is lower than their legal costs of fighting the lawsuit.

It will cost about $25,000 for the insurance company to fight a lawsuit, so they routinely settle claims for that amount without even investigating.

And then you have a reputation for having been sued and having settled out of court.

Insurance is not the answer.

TAXATION

The income earned by the Sole Proprietorship is the personal income of the Sole Proprietor.

It is taxed as personal income.

If it is rental income, it is considered passive income.

It will be reported on Schedule E, Supplemental Income and Loss.

Rental Real Estate is covered in Part I.

Each Schedule E will handle up to three properties. If you have more than that, you use another Schedule E.

The total rental real estate income is transferred to Line 17 on your Form 1040.

I recommend that you get a copy of Schedule E and the Instructions and study them.

Don't worry if you don't completely understand them. Anything is better than nothing.

You can download a Schedule E at:

www.irs.gov/pub/irs-pdf/f1040se.pdf

You can download the Instructions at:

www.irs.gov/pub/irs-pdf/i1040se.pdf

FEDERAL

The Total Income and the Total Expenses of the business are reported on either Schedule C or Schedule E, and the Net Income is then transferred to the Form 1040 Individual Income Tax Return of the Sole Proprietor.

Unlike W-2 wages, where a portion of each check is withheld by the Employer and sent to the IRS for Income Tax liability and Social Security deposits, the Sole Proprietor must send in a Quarterly Estimate of these liabilities directly to the IRS.

The Sole Proprietor is also subject to a 15.3% Self-Employment (SE) Tax unless the income is the passive income of rental activities.

If the business has Employees, there is also Form 941 which must be filed quarterly, and Form 940 which must be filed annually.

If you do not have Employees, and do not have a Qualified Retirement Plan, you are not actually required to have an Employer Identification Number (EIN).

But you should get one anyway.

You don't know when you will be doing business with someone who requires that you provide an EIN.

And, believe me, YOU WILL NOT CONVINCE THEM that you are not required to actually have an EIN, because they DON'T KNOW WHY they are even asking for it. It is just what they have been told to do, and they have been told not to proceed without it.

So, just get one.

You might also feel safer being able to use an EIN instead of putting your Social Security Number out there.

STATE

There are seven States which have no State Income Tax.

They are:

1.) Alaska,

2.) Florida,

3.) Nevada,

4.) South Dakota,

5.) Texas,

6.) Washington, and

7.) Wyoming.

The other States impose some type of tax on income.

The tax rates vary, and the exceptions, exemptions, and thresholds vary.

If you are not already familiar with your State's tax system, go to the State website and read about it.

CONCLUSION

The Sole Proprietorship form of business offers some areas of personal ease and comfort, such as ease of formation, no rules for operation, and easy dissolution.

Those are the advantages.

The disadvantages are many, but the primary one is that the Sole Proprietor is personally liable for all of the obligations of the business.

If the business is sued, the Sole Proprietor will be the one being sued, because the business is not a separate legal entity.

The legal costs alone could be $25,000 or more, even if you win.

If a Judgment is obtained, the Sole Proprietor's personal assets can be seized and sold to satisfy the Judgment.

So, not only could the Sole Proprietor end up broke, but if the personal assets do not provide enough money to pay the entire Judgment, then any assets that the Sole Proprietor acquires in the future can also be taken and sold, until the entire amount of the recorded Judgment has been paid.

Bankruptcy is the only way to escape the situation.

In spite of the tragedy awaiting the Sole Proprietor, a large number of individuals choose to operate with this form of business.

It is a personal choice, and no one can make it for you, but I hope you will think long and hard, and read the rest of this book, before you make your decision.

CHAPTER 2

LIMITED LIABILITY COMPANY

OVERVIEW

Well, there was not much to get excited about in the last Chapter on Sole Proprietorship, but the fact is that there are so few rules and such little structure, there are almost no planning opportunities.

However, the Limited Liability Company (LLC) is totally different.

This is where the fun begins.

The LLC is the best thing to happen to Real Estate Investors since the creation of the Subchapter S Corporation which made it possible to have the protection of a C Corporation without the double taxation.

The Limited Liability Company is created by filing Articles of Organization.

The LLC is owned by the Members.

The ownership can be represented by membership units or just by percentages.

The LLC is managed by either the Members or by one or more persons designated by the Members to be the Manager or Managers.

The agreement between the participants is a contract called the Operating Agreement.

Like the Partnership and the S Corp, the LLC is a Pass-Through Entity (PTE).

See Chapter 13 for an explanation of Pass-Through Entities.

With the LLC, you create a company which you use to do business, and in most States you will have no personal liability arising from the activities of the company, as long as you follow the law.

Now remember, each State has its own laws governing the formation, operation, and dissolution of the Limited Liability Company, which we will now call the LLC.

So, everything that I say should be confirmed by looking at your State law. Most States have very good websites that will give you accurate and current information, and sometimes step-by-step directions for whatever you want to do.

In the Conclusion section at the end of this Chapter, I show you how to find the law for your State.

And I will only be dealing with Real Estate Investors who are doing "Buy and Hold" investing.

If you are flipping properties, you are not investing.

Flipping properties is operating a business, with inventory, and you are a dealer.

I have written an entire Chapter 17 for you.

But you are probably also doing "Buy and Hold," or should be, so this book will be very beneficial to you as well.

FORMATION

There is no Federal law regarding the establishment and operation of a Limited Liability Company (LLC).

LLCs are created under State law, and therefore each one will be a little bit different.

But there are enough similarities that we can refer to all of them in general terms.

ARTICLES OF ORGANIZATION

An LLC is usually formed by filing Articles of Organization with the Secretary of State of your State.

In your State, the document might be called a Certificate of Organization or Certificate of Formation. But, since it is not a "certificate," we will call it Articles of Organization.

The State website for the Secretary of State will have a form with blanks that you can complete and send in with the fee. Or you can use the form as a guide, and draft your own.

A few states require that before you can file your Articles of Organization, you must file a public notice of your intent to do so in the local newspaper.

One person, referred to as the Organizer, can file the papers even if there will be multiple owners.

The information required in the Articles of Organization will vary, but will certainly include:

1.) Name of the LLC.

2.) Address of principal business.

3.) Name(s) of the Member(s).

4.) Name and address of the Registered Agent.

5.) Whether the LLC will be managed by Members or by Managers.

Members can be of any nationality, and there is no limit on the number of Members.

If you intend to operate in a State other than the State in which you form your LLC, you will need to file the necessary documents in the State of operation in order to qualify as a foreign entity. And then you will be required to follow the laws of both States, the one where you formed the LLC, and the one where the LLC is doing business. Usually, the laws of the State of formation will govern the operation of your LLC, but not always. This is something that you need to find out.

The dual-State requirements might also include filing tax returns in multiple States, depending on the requirements of those jurisdictions.

The State where the LLC is formed will also have other laws with which the LLC laws must be coordinated, such as the Community Property laws.

There are nine States with Community Property laws.

1.) Arizona

2.) California

3.) Idaho

4.) Louisiana

5.) Nevada

6.) New Mexico

7.) Texas

8.) Washington

9.) Wisconsin

REGISTERED AGENT

One important decision that you have to make concerns your choice of a Registered Agent.

The Registered Agent is someone, or an Entity, that will be served with the copy of the lawsuit if you are ever sued. You might be tempted to save the fee of having someone else do this, and just act as your own Registered Agent. This is allowed if you are located in the State. But do you want to commit yourself to having a location that is open every business day of the year, because that is the requirement? And do you want a Constable or Process Server showing up at your office when you are meeting with someone? I recommend having a third party handle this.

The Registered Agent's office can also serve as the LLC's "corporate headquarters" if you don't have an office in the State of formation.

You can find a Registered Agent in the State of formation by going to www.registered-agent-information. com, an independent website that contains information on Registered Agents for each State.

OPERATING AGREEMENT

In addition to the Articles of Organization, even if you have only one member, you will need to draft an Operating Agreement.

The Operating Agreement is the heart of your business, and it is the reason that the LLC can be more powerful than any other platform for Real Estate Investing.

The Operating Agreement is the most important of all of your documents.

The Operating Agreement is actually not required by the LLC laws of some States.

This is a huge mistake, and it demonstrates the low level of understanding of the business world by the politicians who created the laws, and their reluctance to listen to people with expertise and experience.

You must have an Operating Agreement.

You must have one even if you are a SMLLC, because later you might want to consider adding a Member, and you need to provide for that.

When you draft the Operating Agreement you want to make sure that you understand exactly how it will be used to control everything that happens in your LLC.

The Operating Agreement will lay out:

1.) Interest ownership of Members.

2.) Rights and responsibilities of Members.

3.) Type of Management.

4.) Allocation of profits.

5.) Manner of holding meetings and voting.

6.) Buyout provisions.

7.) Timeline for profit distributions.

8.) The voting power of Members and Managers.

9.) Limits on disposing of LLC interest.

10.) Member death and disability.

11.) Dispute resolution.

So, you have two decisions to make.

HOW TO DO IT

The first decision is whether to go to the State website and learn about the process of creating an LLC and then doing it yourself, or to pay an online service to do it.

My feeling is that if you actually intend to become a business professional, and are not just playing around, you need to learn all you can about LLCs, and then do the formation yourself.

An online service has no information, education, access, qualifications, or experience that would enable them to do this better than you.

In fact, they have less.

And if you don't do it yourself, you have to think about the fact that, at some point in the future, you could wake up one day and realize that you have about $400,000 of Equity, and about $700,000 of debt obligation inside your LLCs, and you don't even understand how they were set up, or how they work, except the basics.

Do it right from the start.

Learn it, and do it.

But hold up on filing the documents for now.

The second decision you will make concerns your Operating Agreement.

Don't do it yourself.

Learn what an Operating Agreement is, and what it does, and then find an Attorney who practices Real Estate Law, and who has Real Estate Investors as clients.

Know before you go in for your appointment what you want in your Agreement.

Make a list, make a copy.

Then go through the list with the Attorney.

Ask questions, and then ask the Attorney for suggestions.

I think you will be pleasantly surprised to discover what you can do with your Operating Agreement.

After you have the Operating Agreement created for your first LLC, if you continue to use the same Attorney, the Operating Agreement for subsequent LLCs should cost less each time.

You might even get lucky and find an Attorney who will create an Operating Agreement in which most of the variable information will be contained in documents used as attachments attachments which will be referenced in the document as "...as described on Exhibit A which is attached hereto and incorporated herein for all purposes."

A new Operating Agreement can be created much easier.

When you have finished the consultation regarding the Operating Agreement, show the Attorney the documents that you intend to file in order to form the LLC, and go over the documents with him.

Ask questions, and then ask for suggestions.

And I promise you, when your LLC sells the investment property in the future, and you make $170,000 profit, you will not be complaining about the money you paid the Attorney to do it right in the beginning, and you probably will never know how much time and money you saved by doing it right.

FINANCING

The LLC must have money and equipment to operate.

It does not usually start with a bank loan like some other Entities.

The financing will usually come from the future Members of the LLC.

The members will contribute:

1.) cash,

2.) property,

3.) personal services, or

4.) a promise to contribute cash, property, or personal services in the future.

In return for these "Capital Contributions," the LLC Member will receive a percentage of ownership called "Capital Interest."

The LLC can describe the ownership in terms of "membership units" or "ownership percentage."

If membership units are used, these must be described in the Operating Agreement, such as creating 1,000,000 units, and then an investor who puts in 25% of the Capital Interest would receive 250,000 membership units. But this can get cumbersome.

If the LLC is set up for ownership percentage, which is usually the case, the same Member would just be referred to as having 25% ownership percentage, or 25% Capital Interest.

If a Member owns a 25% Capital Interest, that would mean that he would be entitled to 25% of the net sales proceeds if the LLC itself were sold. And if the other Members wanted to buy him out, they would pay him 25% of the total value of the LLC on the books.

Whether or not his 25% Capital Interest would also mean that he will receive 25% of the LLC income and losses depends on the terms written into the Operating Agreement.

CAPITAL CONTRIBUTIONS

Whether the Member contributes cash, property, or services is critical, for him personally, and possibly for the other Members.

The Member will create different tax situations for himself, and possibly other Members, with the IRS, depending on whether he contributes cash, property, or services.

CASH

For the Member who contributes cash, this is not a taxable event, and does not have to be reported on his personal tax return, and no tax liability is incurred. If he contributes $25,000 and receives a 25% Capital Interest, that establishes his tax basis in his Capital Interest at $25,000. If the other Members buy him out a year later for $30,000 before anything else happens to change his Capital Account, he has a $5,000 Capital Gain, which he will report on his tax return and pay taxes.

PERSONAL SERVICES

For the Member who receives his Capital Interest in return for his personal services, the situation is different.

The Member who receives a 25% Capital Interest valued at $25,000 in return for 100 hours of services already performed, and a promise of 400 more hours to be performed, has received "payment for services" under the IRS definition, and is liable for ordinary income taxes on the entire amount.

PROPERTY

For the Member who receives a Capital Interest in return for property, this is a special situation which I cover below in "Contributing Owned Real Estate."

MEMBER INCENTIVES

There is a greater enticement for Members of the LLC to invest in an LLC than there is for Partners to invest in a Partnership or Shareholders to invest in a corporation, because each Member of the LLC can receive different benefits, income and ownership, ones that satisfy their individual needs.

With an S Corp, when the income flows through to the Shareholders and is reported on the Schedule K-1 (1065), the profits and losses are allocated in accordance with the ownership percentages of the Corporation.

If you own 25%, then you are allocated 25% of the profit, or 25% of the losses.

However, the Operating Agreement of the LLC can handle allocations in a flexible manner, without regard to ownership percentages, referred to an Unequal Allocation.

You might have someone interested in becoming a Member who wants to have losses allocated to him, so that he can deduct the amount from other like income and avoid paying taxes on that other income.

Or you might have someone who requires a guaranteed return before the remainder of the LLC income is allocated to the other Members.

The unequal or special allocation is allowed, but must have a "substantial economic effect," according to the IRS.

The IRS says the allocation cannot be <u>only</u> to reduce the Taxpayer's tax obligation.

However, they realize that in most cases, this is the only reason for doing special allocations, and they allow it as long as it has a reasonable business purpose, and as long as all of the taxes tied to the LLC income are being paid by <u>someone.</u>

There are some special requirements regarding each Member's Capital Account and Basis, which I cover below in Bookkeeping.

MANAGEMENT

The Operating Agreement will provide the manner in which the LLC will be managed.

The two possibilities are:

1.) Member Managed, in which all of the Members take part in managing the LLC.

2.) Manager Managed, in which the Members agree on who will do the managing.

Some States require that the designation be made in the Articles of Organization, but the details should always be put into the Operating Agreement.

Under the LLC laws in most States, all Members are equally responsible for the management of the LLC.

This is the "default" classification of "Member Managed."

The Operating Agreement can provide for a different arrangement, and this is one of the most important items in the Operating Agreement.

The different arrangement is the arrangement known as "Manager Managed."

The Member choose one or more persons to manage the LLC, resulting in single management or team management. A non-Member can be chosen as the single manager or as one of the team managers.

Any Member signing the Operating Agreement must understand that if he is not the single Manager, or one of the Managers, he is giving up his right to take part in the management decisions regarding the LLC.

Most of the business disputes that I have seen in the past 30 years involved management disputes, some of them resulting in lawsuits that went on for two or three years, many ending in Bankruptcy for the company, and sometimes for one or both of the individuals.

This is one of the three most important items that you will put into your Operating Agreement, along with ownership division and allocation of income.

Of course, many States have laws (and a good Operating Agreement has provisions) that a Member will always have the right to remove a Manager. If you do not want to be forced to follow the terms of the State law in this regard, the Operating Agreement should spell out exactly what the right is, how and when it can be exercised, and the process for doing it.

It might also be a good idea to provide that the Manager(s) serve for one year, and then must be appointed again.

OPERATING THE BUSINESS

You will operate the business in the most efficient and profitable way you can.

How you do that, and what you will be allowed or required to do, will be detailed in the Operating Agreement of the LLC, and will depend on the type of management you choose.

You should start out with a strong Operating Agreement, and as you go along, and find items that need to be improved, you should amend the Operating Agreement.

It is very important to understand that the LLC can be legally bound to any contract or transaction entered into by any Member in a Member Managed LLC, and by any Manager in a Manager Managed LLC.

Major decisions should only be made at a meeting of the Managers, either a regularly-schedule meeting or one called for the purpose, a "special meeting."

Minutes of the meeting and the votes should be recorded.

The Operating Agreement should spell out when the meeting should be held, who can call a meeting, how notice of the meeting is given, how the voting takes place, what constitutes a quorum, and how many votes are required to pass a proposal under consideration.

Although the State laws do not usually require annual meetings, and your Operating Agreement does not have to contain such a provision, it is a good idea for one of the Members to request a Special Meeting at least annually for the purpose of updating, reviewing, and summarizing operations.

This is not only the responsible thing to do, but it will prevent anyone from later saying, "I didn't know."

Restrictions should be placed on the transfer of Capital Interest in the Operating Agreement.

The Operating Agreement should state that the recipient of a Capital Interest, called the Assignee, regardless of how the Capital Interest was acquired, only receives the "economic interest," which is the distribution of the income.

The Assignee does not receive the management rights, voting rights, or membership rights. You can provide that full membership can be granted to the Assignee by either a majority vote, or a unanimous vote, of the other members.

A SMLLC can add a second Member, or additional Members, as provided for in the Operating Agreement.

This will usually be done by the single Member in a Single Member LLC selling some of his ownership units to one or more persons or Entities, or the LLC itself will just issue additional ownership units and sell them to the new Members.

If a single Member sells units, this will be a taxable transaction, and might require the Member to report the sale and pay taxes.

The LLC selling new units is not a taxable event.

The new Member or Members will sign the Operating Agreement, or an Amended Operating Agreement will be drafted for all Members to sign.

And finally, you should remember when signing documents for the LLC, the signature line should say:

Acme Widgets, LLC

By: _____

John Doe, Member

This will give notice that you are not signing in your capacity as an individual, but that you are signing for the LLC in you capacity as an agent for the LLC.

BUYING REAL ESTATE

The LLC should be created first, and then the real estate should be purchased by the LLC.

You should not purchase the real estate first, and then try to put it into the LLC.

For the reasons why you should not do that, see the following Section on Contributing Owned Real Estate.

FINANCING

The LLC is a separate Business Entity and should purchase the real estate and hold the real estate in the name of the LLC.

If the LLC is new, and it probably will be, and you are not paying cash for the property, it will be difficult, and maybe impossible, to get a mortgage in the name of the LLC.

However, there are Lenders who will loan money to the LLC and take the real estate as security on the loan, if the Loan-to-Value (LTV) ratio is low enough.

It might require a larger Down Payment by the LLC, and it might require a guarantee of the loan by one or more Members of the LLC.

But don't be afraid of guarantees, and just remember that there are two types of guarantees.

The first is a Loan Guarantee, where you sign an agreement with the Lender that if the loan goes into default, the Lender will simply notify you, and it is your responsibility to deal with the problem. This is virtually the same as getting the loan yourself.

The second is a Guaranty Agreement, where you guarantee the Lender that you will cover any loss suffered if the loan goes into default, the Lender forecloses, and does not realize enough net proceeds to pay the loan.

The second is obviously better.

But if the Lender insists that you sign the Note, look for another Lender.

SEGREGATING PROPERTY

You should always hold each of your rental properties in a separate LLC.

If you believe that $1,500 is too much to pay for the most important item in your entire real estate investing plan, then you don't understand yet what matters and what doesn't.

If you have been investing for a few years, and you have three properties, all in the same LLC, and one tenant has an accident on your stairs, and is paralyzed for life, the lawsuit will probably result in a Judgment in the millions of dollars.

The lawsuit will be against the LLC, as will the Judgment, and all of the properties will be foreclosed on and sold to pay toward the Judgment lien.

Even without considering the possibility of a lawsuit, there are other reasons to put each property into its own LLC.

The income and losses from the rental real estate are passive in nature.

If you put only one property into each LLC, the losses from one LLC are deductible from the income of the other LLCs, shielding that income from taxation.

This significant advantage might allow you to take on a good long-term investment that will incur early losses, when other investors might not be able to do so.

It also allows you to balance your risks, as well as isolating them.

When the downturn comes, and some of your investments start to go belly-up, you have built a firewall between the shaky investments and the better investments that might survive. If you have to chuck the bad ones, you can still save the good ones.

If you had them all in one LLC, they might all go down.

To look at it from the opposite perspective, there is really no good reason to put all of you properties into one LLC, except to save money. And if you can't afford the best liability protection available, maybe you shouldn't be in the business.

Risking everything you own to save $1,500 just does not make sense.

CONTRIBUTING OWNED REAL ESTATE

As I discussed above in FINANCING, one of the ways that a Member can receive a Capital Interest in the LLC is in return for property.

This can be a tax nightmare!

PRACTICAL CONSIDERATIONS

But first, before we get to the tax considerations, there are simple, practical reasons why you should not transfer title to real estate to the LLC in return for your Capital Interest.

1.) The property probably has debt, for which you are personally liable, and which is being secured by a lien on the property, title to which is in your name.

You cannot transfer the title without transferring the debt, and the Lender is not likely to agree to that.

If the Lender does agree to it, the Lender would probably require that you remain liable on the debt, or a Guarantor for it, and that means that you are now responsible for a share of the LLC's debt, and that causes other IRS regulations to kick in.

2.) When you acquired the property, you obtained an Owner's Title Insurance Policy which guarantees that the property has clear title, and promises to cover any losses caused by defective title.

If the property has a mortgage, when you bought it, the Lender received a Mortgagee's Title Insurance Policy which insured the Lender against loss for the same causes related to title.

When you transfer ownership, both of these insurance policies cease, and neither the LLC nor the Lender is covered for things like a gas pipeline easement being discovered under the property.

If you decide to go ahead anyway, let's look at the tax nightmare ahead.

TAX CONSIDERATIONS

Usually, the property that you transfer to the LLC has gone up in value since you acquired it. (You would have to wonder why the LLC is accepting real estate if it is going down in value.)

Therefore, you are transferring what is called "appreciated property."

If you bought the property for $25,000 and it is worth $100,000 at the time of transfer, you will receive a Capital Interest equal to $100,000.

But, your tax basis in your Capital Interest of $100,000 will be $25,000.

The transfer itself does not trigger the Capital Gains tax. But you will have to pay the Capital Gains tax when you sell your Capital Interest, or when the LLC is sold.

However, if you receive a profit distribution from the LLC within two years of the date of the property transfer, you might owe the Capital Gains tax at that time.

You might also owe the Capital Gains tax if the LLC itself sells the property you contributed, or distributes the property to another Member.

The situation becomes even more complicated if you transfer property to the LLC and the property has mortgage debt attached to it.

This is not a problem for a Single Member LLC, although there are strong reasons not to do it, as described above.

But there are immediate tax consequences for a Member who transfers property with mortgage debt to the Multi Member LLC.

When this happens, the mortgage debt is allocated among all of the LLC Members, including the transferor.

This has the effect of increasing each Member's basis in his Capital Interest, which will decrease his Capital Gains tax later when he sells his interest.

But it can have an immediate, and negative, effect on the transferor Member.

If he is in a Multi Member LLC with four other members and he transfers real estate with a FMV of $150,000 and which still has a $100,000 mortgage balance, that personal debt will now be shared among the five Members.

That means that he is no longer liable for $80,000 of the mortgage.

The result is that he will have $80,000 of personal "debt relief," and the IRS will consider this taxable as ordinary income to the transferor if the debt being transferred exceeds the total of:

a.) the transferor's share of the LLC debt, and

b.) the basis of the real estate being contributed.

If the transferor had a $70,000 basis in the transferred property, this is a taxable event.

Not only that, but he received a $150,000 Capital Interest when he transferred the property, so when he sells his Capital Interest, he will owe Capital Gains on another $80,000 even if he doesn't sell it for more than $150,000.

If he does, he will owe Capital Gains on that profits as well.

SELLING REAL ESTATE

The real estate is owned by the LLC, and will have to be sold by the LLC.

The Operating Agreement of the LLC will detail who has the authority to make the decision to sell the real estate, and will describe the steps necessary to accomplish it.

The Net Sales Proceeds from selling the real estate will be owned by the LLC.

The "nature" of the income, for tax purposes, will be Capital Gains.

If the real estate was held for a year or less, the Capital Gains will be Short-Term Capital Gains.

If the real estate was held for at least a year and a day, the Capital Gains will be Long-Term Capital Gains.

Since the LLC is a Pass-Through Entity (PTE), the income will come to the Member or Members as Capital Gains to be reported on their individual tax returns.

PROVIDING SERVICES

The services that you will be providing to the LLC as a Member Manager will not be paid for with a paycheck.

Your LLC will operate as a Pass-Through Entity (PTE) and all of the income, deductions, credits and other items will pass through to the Members and be reported on their individual tax returns.

This will represent their compensation for managing the business, as well as the return on their investment of funds and of time putting the company together.

See Chapter 13 Pass-Through Entities for a complete explanation.

DISTRIBUTIVE SHARE

You should become familiar with a term that the IRS uses in its rules and publications, because you will see it a lot.

"Distributive share."

The Distributive Share is the amount of an LLC's annual profits and losses that will be allocated to each Member.

Usually, the Distributive Share is the same as the Member's Capital Interest.

For Example, if four people each own 25% Capital Interest in the LLC, each would be allocated 25% of the LLC's profits and losses.

But the Operating Agreement can provide for a different allocation, and this is called "unequal allocation."

For Example, one of the four Members has 30 years experience operating the type of business and has been very successful, and will be more valuable, and he will be assigned 40% of the profits and losses, and the other three Members will be assigned 20% each.

The IRS requires that the Unequal Allocation must have a "substantial economic effect," in addition to any effect on the Member's tax liability, but this applies primarily in situations where one Member is allocated all of the losses so that he can deduct them from his other similar income. If you are doing this, it would be a good idea to consult an expert. It is complicated.

PAID COMPENSATION

It is possible in the Operating Agreement to have conditions whereby one of the Members receives a Special Allocation in the nature of an Unequal Allocation, but actually before the computation of the income which is subject to the Unequal Allocation.

So you have a Special Allocation, and then an Unequal Allocation of the rest.

There might be one Member Manager who shows up every day, executes the business plans, and ensures that tasks are completed, all things that the other Members do not do, and he is therefore entitled to compensation.

But to deal with this situation with a Special Allocation, as cool as it sounds, can really cause problems among the Members. There is a very high likelihood that at least one other Member will feel that the compensated Member is not spending sufficient time to justify the Special Allocation of income, and all of the Members will constantly be aware that the one Member's payment is coming from LLC income, before they get their share.

You could even have a situation where the Special Allocation takes up all of the income, and the other Members get nothing.

A much better solution is to have the Member who is providing these services to actually be an employee of the business, totally separate from his status as a Member and his position as a Member Manager.

He will receive a salary, and it will be treated as a regular business expense, just like the telephone, internet service, office supplies, etc., and when the LLC income is calculated, it will be distributed the way that everyone agreed in the Operating Agreement.

BOOKKEEPING

Bookkeeping has two purposes in your business.

The primary purpose of Bookkeeping is to keep track of the income and expenses, and to file the required tax documents.

You can learn to do this yourself fairly easily, or you can just find a good Bookkeeper to start with, and maintain frequent communications so that you always know where you are.

But the secondary purpose of Bookkeeping for LLCs, LPs, and S Corps is to keep track of each owner's Capital Account.

This requires following the standard rules of accounting (which you are probably familiar with, whether you realize it or not), but also following the specific IRS regulations (with which you are probably not familiar).

A Capital Account shows the amount of money put into the company by the investor/owner, plus his allocated portion of the profits, and minus the distributions that he has received.

If the Capital Account goes negative, the owner can be required to bring it to zero.

And, of course, he must bring it to zero before he can sell his interest, or in the event of a dissolution of the entity.

Capital Account reconciliation might not be something that you want to be spending your time doing, and might be a good reason for you to hire a Bookkeeper.

If the Operating Agreement provides for unequal allocation of the income, deductions, credits and other items, the Bookkeeping must take this into account.

You must also keep track of Basis.

"Basis" is generally what you paid for an asset.

For LLCs and LPs, the concept of "Basis" can become complicated.

You will have "Inside Basis" and you will have "Outside Basis."

First, Inside Basis.

The Entity will purchase an asset. The purchase price is the Entity's basis in the asset. The Entity might spend money to improve the asset. This cost is added, creating a new Basis. The Entity might be entitled to deduct a portion of the Basis as a "Depreciation Allowance." This is deducted, and will create a new Basis.

This is the Inside Basis, the Basis that the Entity has in the assets.

Now, Outside Basis.

The Owners of the Entity will also have a Basis in the ownership of the Entity that they acquire, their ownership interest.

If there are two Owners and they each invest $30,000 to become partners in the Entity, each Owner would have a $30,000 Basis in their interest in the Entity.

The Outside Basis can be increased if the Entity secures a loan and the loan is personally guaranteed by the Owners. This is different from an S Corp, where the Outside Basis can only be increased if the Owner loans the money to the Entity.

LIABILITY

"Limited Liability Company" does not mean that the company has limited liability.

The company is completely liable for all of its activities. And if those activities result in an injury to someone, and that person obtains a judgment against the company, the company's asset can be taken to satisfy the judgment.

The "limited liability" in Limited Liability Company refers to the fact that the owners/investors (Members) of the LLC are not liable for the obligations of the LLC, except to the extent of the amount that they have invested.

That is because this invested amount now belongs to the LLC, and if it is lost and there are still unsatisfied obligation of the LLC, the owners/investors are not liable for those obligations.

The "liability" for the operation of the "company" is "limited" for the owners/investors to the amount that the owners/investors have put into the LLC.

ENTITY

The Limited Liability Company is responsible for its own debts and obligations.

The LLC can be sued if it does not pay these debts and meet these obligations, and the assets of the LLC can be sold to satisfy the debts and obligations.

But the Members are not liable.

However, a claimant can attempt to "pierce the veil" of the company, ignore its existence, or dissolve it, and hold the individual Members liable under certain circumstances.

That discussion is very complicated, and is different for each State, because it depends on the law of each individual State, and we don't have the space for a complete discussion here.

It is a rare occurrence to "pierce the veil," and usually involves wrongdoing on the part of a Member.

It gets more attention and publicity than is warranted by the frequency of its occurrence.

I refer you to Chapter 19 on Charging Orders for some understanding of how outside liability can lead to dissolving the LLC.

INDIVIDUAL

The Members of the LLC are not liable for the debts and obligations of the LLC, except, of course, for any amount of debt that they have personally guaranteed.

Also, an individual Member might be held liable for any negligent personal acts that result in damages being awarded against the LLC. However, other LLC Members will not share the liability. It will only be assessed against the LLC and the responsible Member. The LLC insurance policy might or might not cover the negligent act of the individual Member.

And the interest owned by the Member in the LLC cannot be taken to satisfy the Member's individual obligations, except in a few States, and in narrow circumstances in some other States.

I refer you to the discussion of Charging Orders in Chapter 19 for an explanation of how this works.

There is one way that an individual who is a Member of an LLC can be held liable for the obligations of the LLC, and that concerns the IRS.

If you are the individual responsible for sending in the money withheld from employees' paychecks, and you fail to do so, you will be held personally liable by the IRS, even if you were told to do so by the other Members.

And this is not just a fine.

This can become a Federal Tax Lien on everything you own or ever will own, including wages, until it is paid.

TAXATION

The two main reason for using an LLC are protection against personal liability, and control of your tax obligations.

After you create the LLC and are receiving the protection against personal liability, you then get to decide how you want to be taxed by the IRS.

FEDERAL

There are actually two ways in which you can tell the IRS how you want to have the LLC treated for tax purposes.

The first way is to do nothing.

If you do nothing, and you are the only Member of the LLC, the IRS will treat you for tax purposes as an individual taxpayer and you will report your business activities on your personal tax return, either Schedule E or Schedule C.

The IRS considers the LLC "a disregarded entity."

If the LLC has more than one Member, and the Members do nothing, the LLC will be treated for tax purposes as a partnership.

The second way to tell the IRS how you want to have the LLC treated for tax purposes is to file Form 8832, Entity Classification Election.

For a Single Member LLC, the Member can elect to be treated as "an association taxed as a corporation" as the language of the Form says. This means that you are electing to be treated as a C Corporation.

If you want to be treated as an S Corporation, you must follow the filing of Form 8832 with filing Form 2553, Election by a Small Business Corporation and that will make you an S Corp.

NOTE: there is language in the Form 8832 Instructions that seems to say that if you are an LLC and you only file the Form 2553 without filing the Form 8832, you will be "deemed" to have first filed the Form 8832. But I don't like it, and I think it could cause big problems under certain circumstances. I strongly recommend filing both forms. I have a more complete explanation below.

For a Multiple Member LLC, you can file Form 8832 and Form 2553 just like a Single Member LLC.

At the federal tax level, your LLC will not file a tax return and pay taxes, unless you file Form 8832, Entity Classification Election, and elect to be taxed as a C Corporation, and do not also file Form 2553, Election by a Small Business Corporation.

But your LLC might still be required to file a federal income tax return, and pass the income through to the owners, since the LLC is a Pass-Through Entity (PTE).

ENTITY

Form 8832 is not specifically for LLCs.

According to the IRS, it is for use by any "eligible entity" to "elect how it will be classified for federal tax purposes, as a corporation, a partnership, or as an entity disregarded as separate from its owner."

The LLC is an "eligible entity" entitled to file Form 8832.

If you are a single owner, the form says:

"You can elect to be classified as an association taxable as a corporation or to be disregarded as a separate entity." By "you" it means the LLC.

For a Multi Member LLC, the form says:

"You can elect to be classified as a partnership or an association taxable as a corporation."

The Instructions to Form 8832 say that if you do not file anything, the single owner LLC will be classified as a disregarded entity, and the multiple owner LLC will be classified as a partnership.

Then, at this point, I believe that the IRS has introduced confusion into the situation.

An Entity that wants to taxed as an S Corp should, I believe, reasonably take the first step of filing Form 8832 and "elect to be classified as an association taxable as a corporation" and then file Form 2553, Election by a Small Business Corporation to be taxed as an S Corp.

But in a small paragraph on page 2 of the Form 8832 Instructions, it says:

"An eligible entity that timely files Form 2553 to elect classification as an S corporation and meets all other requirements to qualify as an S corporation is deemed to have made an election under Regulations section 301.7701-3(c)(v) to be classified as an association taxable as a corporation."

Then, section 301.7701-3(c)(v) says:

"An eligible entity that timely elects to be an S corporation under section 1362(a)(1) is treated as having made an election under this section to be classified as an association, provided that (as of the effective date of the election under section 1362(a)(1)) the entity meets all other requirements to qualify as a small business corporation under section 1361(b). Subject to § 301.7701-3(c)(1)(iv), the deemed election to be classified as an association will apply as of the effective date of the S corporation election and will remain in effect until the entity makes a valid election, under § 301.7701-3(c)(1)(i), to be classified as other than an association."

There is nothing in the consent statement of Form 2553 signed by the owners informing the owners that they are "deemed" to have filed another, different, Form, and I think that if the S Corp status was ever lost, and the LLC was reverted to being a C Corporation, even though a Form 8832 was never signed under oath and filed by the owners, there could be problems.

Form 2553 is for use by "a small business corporation" and an LLC that has not elected corporate taxation status is not "a small business corporation."

I just don't understand why the IRS sets up this elaborate, confusing, convoluted, and very unclear process for being "deemed" to have filed Form 8832, when you can just file the damn Form in fifteen minutes, and not have any of this uncertainty.

I always file both Forms, and I am not aware of any recent cases where this has become an issue, so you can make up your own mind about whether to file only Form 2553 if you want to be taxed as an S Corp.

So, as you can see, the LLC will not pay Federal Income Taxes unless you first elect to be treated for tax purposes as a C Corporation, and then you do not file the Form 2553 Election to be treated as a Subchapter S Corporation.

If you choose to be taxed as a C Corporation, you will file Form 1120, US Corporation Income Tax Return, and pay the appropriate amount of corporate tax, which is now 21% under the new Tax Cuts And Jobs Act. You will transfer the remainder of the income into a corporate account called Retained Earnings.

If you decide to pay a Dividend to the Shareholder(s), this is where it comes from.

But if you are an individual and you just create your LLC, and then do nothing about filing your Form 8832, Entity Classification Election, then you will receive the default classification, which is Disregarded Entity.

Being classified for tax purposes as a Disregarded Entity means that for purposes of reporting the income and paying the taxes, it is the same as if you owned the property in your individual name.

The rental income will be reported on your Schedule E, and the LLC will file nothing with the IRS.

If the LLC has more than one owner, it will not be a Disregarded Entity, but will be considered a Partnership.

The LLC will than file a Form 1065, US Return of Partnership Income, and then provide a Schedule K-1 (Form 1065) for each Partner, showing each Partner's share of income, deductions, credits, and other items, which the Partner will report on his personal return.

MICHAEL LANTRIP

I have a good discussion of the Form 1065 handling of Partners' Account in Chapter 6 Limited Partnership > Taxation > Federal > Entity.

If the LLC elects to be classified for tax purposes as an S Corp, it will file Form 1120S, US Income Tax Return for an S Corporation, which is similar to the Form 1120 that is filed by C Corporations.

The Form 1120S will calculate the income, credits and deductions, and put them on a Schedule K-1 for each owner, and the individual owner will report the amount on their personal tax returns.

INDIVIDUAL

If you choose to have the LLC treated for tax purposes as a Disregarded Entity, the income and expenses will be reported on your Schedule E and the Net Income will be added to your Form 1040.

This income will be taxed as ordinary income at your individual tax rate.

The income will not be subject to Self-Employment (SE) Tax because it is considered to be passive income, and therefore unearned income.

If you elect to have your LLC treated as an S Corporation, you will receive a Schedule K-1 (1120S), which will give you all of the numbers to use on your tax return, along with instructions about where to put them.

If you perform services for the S Corp, you will have to be paid a reasonable salary, and that salary will be subject to withholding for Social Security and Medicare, half of which will be paid by the Corporation and half withheld from your check.

If your LLC has more than one owner, it will be treated for tax purposes as a partnership, and you will receive a Schedule K-1 (1065) showing your share of the income, deductions, credits, and other items, which you will report on your personal income tax return.

If you are a Disregarded Entity, an S Corp, or a Partnership, the income that is passed through to you qualifies for the Section 199A 20% Qualified Business Income Exclusion.

See Chapter 13 Pass-Through Entities, and Chapter 14 Qualified Business Income for a complete discussion of this.

You will not be able to form your LLC in a State that has no income tax, and thereby avoid paying State taxes where you reside.

Remember, the LLC is a Pass-Through Entity and you will report the income on your personal tax return.

And you are required to file your personal tax return where your "tax home" is, and that is your State of residence.

STATE

There are seven States which have no State Income Tax.

They are:

1.) Alaska,

2.) Florida,

3.) Nevada,

4.) South Dakota,

5.) Texas,

6.) Washington, and

7.) Wyoming.

The other States impose some type of tax on income.

The tax rates vary, and the exceptions, deductions, exemptions, and thresholds vary.

Most State will treat the LLC the say way that the IRS does for tax purposes, but might have some additional filing requirements.

You should go to your State's taxation website to find out.

ENTITY

Each State will treat LLC income differently, depending on how you elect to be taxed at the federal level.

Your State website will contain the information you need to deal with this.

INDIVIDUAL

Each State will treat LLC income differently, depending on how you elect to be taxed at the federal level.

Your State website will contain the information you need to deal with this.

CONCLUSION

The Limited Liability Company is the favorite business entity of most small businesses, but especially real estate investors.

The LLC is a total departure from the old way of doing business, and with the new Tax Cuts and Jobs Act, it is likely to become the overwhelming choice of the future.

In addition to what we have already discussed, there are three major advantages that the LLC has over other Entities.

FLEXIBILITY

You can use an LLC for almost any situation that your are likely to encounter as a real estate investor, and still not have to sacrifice benefits for anyone.

Whether your LLC has one Member, two or three Members, or 100 Members, you can write the Operating Agreement to do exactly what you want to do, the way you want to do it.

You can override almost all of the rules contained in the LLC statutes of your State.

ASSET PROTECTION

The LLC is the ideal way to own real estate, for two reasons.

The two reasons also provide dual liability protection.

If your real estate is owned by your LLC and there is an accident on the premises that results in a lawsuit leading to a large Judgment, the Judgment will be against the LLC, and not against you personally.

To satisfy the Judgment, on the assets of the LLC, the real estate, can be taken.

And the assets must be taken subject to the existing debt, which is paid off when the asset is sold.

The only thing you lose will be your Equity. And if you are careful and make sure that you carry as much debt as possible on the real estate, this will prevent the LLC from even being sued in the first place, because there is not enough equity to justify the time and expense of a lawsuit.

The second scenario involves a lawsuit and Judgment against you, or another Member of the LLC, not the LLC itself.

The LLC is unique among Business Entities in this regard, because the real estate owned by the LLC cannot be taken by the holder of the Judgment Lien.

Also, the Member's ownership of his interest in the LLC cannot be taken to satisfy the Judgment Lien.

The only remedy available to the holder of the Judgment Lien is to have the Court award a Charging Order, which entitles the Judgment Lien holder to receive the distributions of income, if such distributions are made.

But the holder of the Judgment Lien, the recipient named in the Charging Order, will still be required to pay income taxes on the amount of the annual distributions, even if they are not distributed.

As you can see, this will likely prevent the Judgment Lien holder from even requesting a Charging Order.

And since the Judgment Lien holder does not receive the rights of the Member of the LLC, even with a Charging Order, and cannot take part in the operation of the company, there will probably not even be a lawsuit if you hold all of your assets in different LLCs.

RAISING CAPITAL

The general impression is that Startup Entrepreneurs and Investors only use C Corps for investing purposes.

This is true if the amounts are in the millions and multi-millions of dollars.

But for at least 90% of such projects, which are much smaller, the LLC is the perfect platform and Entity.

This is true for both the Entrepreneur and the Investor.

Investors love the "pass-through" nature of the Partnership tax treatment.

The income is passive income and not subject to the 15.3% Self-Employment tax, and up to 20% of the total might even be tax-free under Section 199A.

The losses are deductible from the Investors' other passive income, allowing them to actually deduct their investment from taxable income.

For the Entrepreneur, the Operating Agreement can be written so that Investors can get exactly what they want in return for their funds, so it is much easier to attract capital.

The LLC can have an unlimited number of Investors, and they can be located anywhere.

The LLC can even have different classes of Membership, some with voting rights and some without, some with the right to transfer ownership, some without.

The Entrepreneur can also provide in the Operating Agreement that he will be the sole Member Manager, and he will be able to run the project on his own instead of having to hold up every decision until all Members have been notified, have reviewed the material, and have held a meeting to vote their approval.

The LLC can be just like running your own project, using other people's money, without dealing with stock, or Limited Partnership interests, or using a scammy Trust.

I think I have provided everything you will need as a Real Estate Investor to make your decision about whether the LLC is the Best Business Entity for you, but there are always additional items that you want to know about.

The best place for you to learn about those things is your own State's website.

Go to www.statelocalgov.net.

In the left sidebar, click the down arrow for "Select Topic" and choose SOS (for Secretary of State).

You will be shown a list of the States. Scroll down to yours and click on the Secretary of State link.

Use the Search box to find what you need.

If you want to look at your State's law governing LLCs, or even another State's laws, go to soswy.state. wy.us/Business.

This is Wyoming's website, and it is the best one of it kind I have ever seen.

Under the Section "Maintaining Your Business" click on "50 States' Business Information" and then click on your State in the map.

CHAPTER 3

C CORPORATION

OVERVIEW

Before we deal with the S Corporation, I want to deal with the C Corporation.

It will improve your understanding of the S Corporation later on.

The standard corporation is called a "C Corporation" because it is created under Subchapter C of the Internal Revenue Code.

It is commonly referred to as a C Corp.

The C Corp is run by a group of Officers, usually a President, one or more Vice Presidents, a Secretary, and a Treasurer.

In recent years we are hearing about the CEO, the CFO, the CTO, and the COO.

"CEO" stands for "Chief Executive Officer."

This should mean that there are a number of other "Executive Officers," and the CEO is the Chief one of them. But usually, there are no other Executive Officers.

The term "CEO" is just being used because it sounds impressive.

He is actually what has always been referred to in the business world as the President of the company.

If there are other people over whom he has authority, they are probably the equivalent of Vice Presidents, each with a specific area of authority, such as Vice President for Finance.

"CFO" stands for "Chief Financial Officer."

"CTO" stands for "Chief Technical Officer."

And I don't know what a "COO" is.

Of course, a C Corp can be structured in any way that the organizers want to structure it.

If they want the Treasurer to be called the Chief Financial Officer (CFO), then that is what they do.

The Bylaws of the C Corp will explain the titles and duties of everyone.

But from the standpoint of structure, the company is run by the Officers, whatever they are called.

The Officers are also employees of the C Corp.

The Officers are chosen by the Board of Directors.

While the Officers run the corporation, the Board of Directors make the decisions about how the corporation should be run, and select the people to run it.

The Board of Directors are elected by the Shareholders.

And here's where the real control of the C Corp comes in.

The Shareholders own the stock issued by the corporation, and therefore, the Shareholders own the corporation.

They elect individuals to be Directors who will carry out the Shareholders' wishes about how the corporation should be run.

And those Directors choose the Officers to carry out the day-to-day operation in accordance with the wishes of the Shareholders.

FORMATION

The statutes concerning the formation and operation of a C Corp are different in each of the fifty States.

The C Corp is not a federal Entity; it is a State Entity.

The method of formation, however, is similar.

The Incorporator, also called the Organizer, files a document called Articles of Incorporation, or maybe Articles of Organization, with the Secretary of State of the State in which the corporation will be based.

The information required to be in the Articles will vary, but will usually include the name of the corporation, the address, the name of the Organizer or Initial Director, and the number of shares of stock authorized.

In addition, the Articles will contain the name and address of a Registered Agent, someone who will be authorized to receive all legal notifications on behalf of the corporation.

The Articles will be the only document required to be filed in the public records.

But in addition to the Articles, the organizing corporation will draft Corporate Bylaws.

The Bylaws are the rules for the internal operation of the corporation, and are not made public, but describe all of the processes for such things as issuing stock, electing the Board of Directors, the titles of the Officers, what their responsibilities will be, and how they will be chosen.

The corporation will be authorized to issue a specific number of shares of stock in the Bylaws, usually one million shares, and these are called Authorized Shares.

The Organizer (or Initial Director) will hold an Organization Meeting and carry out the directions contained in the Bylaws to activate the corporation.

This will usually include the issuance of a portion of the stock to individuals identified in the Bylaws.

The shares will be issued either at a stipulated Part Value, or at No Par Value, but for a stipulated price.

Once the stock is issued, the Shareholders will elect the Board of Directors, and the Board of Directors will choose the Officers.

We now have a C Corp and it is being run by the Officers, usually with the President in charge.

FINANCING

A C Corp cannot pay an Attorney to draft the documents necessary to establish the corporation, nor pay the filing fee required to file the documents, because the C Corp does not exist at that point.

So, the Organizer pays the Attorney and then pays the filing fee, and has the Attorney provide in the Bylaws that the President of the corporation is authorized to reimburse the Organizer for the legal expenses and filing fees from the money that the corporation will receive from the issue of shares of stock.

If a single person creates the corporation, for Example, then at this point the C Corp will have a single Shareholder in complete control of the corporation.

The corporation will usually issue a portion of the authorized shares, about 100,000 and these will be referred to as Issued and Outstanding Shares.

The stock will be issued at a specific Par Value stipulated in the Bylaws, or will be issued with No Par Value, but at the price stipulated in the Bylaws.

If the shares are issued at $1.00, then the corporation will begin operation with one or more Shareholders owning all of the stock of the corporation and with an initial capitalization of $100,000.

From this point on, the C Corp is a legal entity and can either borrow more money on its own, or can sell more shares of stock.

MANAGEMENT

The management of the C Corp is done by the Officers.

Of course, the Officers are elected by the Board of Directors, and will usually be doing what the Board of Directors wants done, and in the way in which they want it done.

And since the Board of Directors is elected by the Shareholders, it is the Shareholders who control the management of the C Corp.

When smaller corporations are created, including one with a single Shareholder, the Shareholder is usually the President, Chairman of the Board of Directors, and the only one voting on anything because he owns all of the stock and is the only Director.

Some States require that the corporation have a position of Secretary for signing certain documents, in addition to those that must be signed by the President, but these States also allow the same person to hold both positions.

So that person will be elected to the position of President/Secretary.

In two-person corporations, one will hold the position of President/Treasurer and the other will be Vice President/Secretary.

OPERATING THE BUSINESS

As I said, the President pretty much runs the company.

The President will hire and supervise the employees.

There are some actions, such as the manner of purchasing or selling real estate, which might have to be done by a Resolution from the Board of Directors, and these actions are dictated by the terms contained in the Bylaws of the Corporation.

But for most things, the C Corp is run just like any other business.

Decisions are made by the President, and carried out by the other Officers and employees.

BUYING REAL ESTATE

Real Estate is purchased in the name of the corporation.

It can be purchased with cash from the capital of the corporation, or with a Down Payment and financing from a Lender.

The debt on the Real Estate will be the obligation of the corporation, and there will be no personal liability for the Officers, Directors, or Shareholders.

The President will sign the documents with his own name, followed by "President, ABC Corporation" to show that he is not signing as an individual, but in his capacity as the agent of the corporation.

CONTRIBUTING OWNED REAL ESTATE

People like the idea of creating a corporation and then "transferring" property into it.

It sounds cool.

But it can be a nightmare of complexity.

It raises too many questions. What is the value of the property? What is your Basis in the property? How much stock did you receive? Is this a taxable transaction? What is the value of the property on the corporate books?

You probably don't know the answers to all of these questions, and some of them might not have answers.

And yet, you will need to determine all of these things, and more, if you try to set up a corporation and transfer property into it.

So, how do you get your real estate into the corporation?

The easiest way, and the simplest way, is usually the best way.

You sell the real estate to the corporation for $X and you receive a Promissory Note from the corporation in return. As long as the price is at or near the market value, and the terms of the transaction are "in the ordinary course of business," this is a legitimate "arms length" transaction and will meet IRS approval.

If you sell the property for more than your Basis, you report the transaction on your personal tax return and you pay the Capital Gains tax. Alternatively, you can treat the transaction as an Installment Sale, and only report the profit portion of the payments as received.

The real estate goes onto the company books at the purchase price, and the depreciable portion is depreciated for the appropriate period.

The corporation will make payments to you and will be able to deduct the interest portion of the payments as an expense.

You receive the payments and report the interest portion as income.

If you paid all of your Capital Gains tax up front, the principal portion of the payments are not taxable to you.

SELLING REAL ESTATE

If the real estate is sold, the corporation will be the Seller because the corporation is the Owner.

The corporation will be liable for the tax on the Capital Gains and the Depreciation Recapture.

The selling of real estate might be one of the acts where the Bylaws require a Corporate Resolution signed by the Board of Directors, but the Deed can be signed by the President of the corporation in that capacity.

PROVIDING SERVICES

If you are a Shareholder, Director, or Officer of a corporation, you can provide your personal services to the corporation and not trigger any requirements as to wages or withholding.

Since the income of the corporation does not "pass-through" to you, it is not considered non-self-employment income, like it would if this were an S Corp, and there is no other requirements.

If you are in control of the corporation, you can either pay yourself a salary or not, depending on what your plan is for your Estate Planning and retirement.

That is a discussion for you to have with your tax advisor.

BOOKKEEPING

The books of a corporation are kept the same way that they are for any other business.

You will create a monthly Income Statement and Balance Sheet.

If you have employees, you will file the Quarterly Reports and the Annual Reports regarding the Social Security Withholding and the Income Tax Withholding, along with other miscellaneous amounts for items like unemployment insurance.

Operating rental real estate activities in a C Corp means that the income is business income, and is taxed at the corporate tax rate of 21%.

There is no Qualified Business Income Exclusion of 20% like there is with Pass-Through Entities.

LIABILITY

Liability, at least in the personal sense, is not a consideration with a C Corp.

The Shareholders, Directors, and Officers have no personal liability related to the operation of the corporation.

Directors are sometimes sued in their individual capacity when a corporation is sued.

Although such actions are seldom successful, a good set of Bylaws will usually provide that the corporation will defend, and indemnify if necessary, the Officers and Directors if this happens.

ENTITY

The C Corp is totally liable for the actions of the corporation, as any legal entity is.

INDIVIDUAL

The individual, whether a Shareholder, Director, or Officer of the corporation has no personal liability for the actions of the corporation.

TAXATION

The C Corp is taxed at the corporate level by both the IRS, and by the States that have a corporate income tax.

FEDERAL

At the federal level, the C Corp will file the Form 1120 US Corporate Income Tax Return.

The corporate tax rate is 21%.

ENTITY

The C Corp reports its annual income on Form 1120 U.S. Corporate Income Tax Return.

INDIVIDUAL

The individual Shareholder has no liability for the taxability of corporate income.

If the C Corp pays a dividend to the Shareholder, the dividend is reported on Schedule B of the individual's Form 1040 tax return.

STATE

There are seven States which have no State Income Tax.

They are:

1.) Alaska,

2.) Florida,

3.) Nevada,

4.) South Dakota,

5.) Texas,

6.) Washington, and

7.) Wyoming.

The other States impose some type of tax on income.

The tax rates vary, and the exceptions, exemptions, and thresholds vary.

ENTITY

If the C Corp is required to file a State income tax return, it will be very similar to the Federal income tax return.

Some States will give a credit for the same tax paid at the Federal level.

Each State's tax laws are different and cannot be recounted here, but each State usually has an excellent website, with all of the information and forms that you will need.

INDIVIDUAL

The individual Shareholder has no tax liability for the income of the C Corp.

If the individual receives a Dividend from the C Corp, that dividend will be reported on the individual's State income tax return.

CONCLUSION

It is rare for rental real estate to be owned in a C Corp.

The LLC and the S Corp are more popular choices.

The primary advantage of the C Corp as a form of business is that it has been around for so long that there are no questions about how it is formed and operated. All of those questions have been answered by the many Court cases of the past hundred years.

CHAPTER 4

SUBCHAPTER S CORPORATION

OVERVIEW

The Subchapter S Corporation is probably the second most popular business entity for real estate investing.

If you are confused by exactly what a Subchapter S Corporation is, the reason for that confusion could be that much of what is on the internet, and some of what is in books currently on the market, is simply not correct.

So this is a good time to clear the deck and explain exactly what we are talking about.

At one time, before lawmakers screwed things up with the way they created the framework of the Limited Liability Company, there was only one type of corporation.

There still is, and I will explain in a minute, but many people think that there are two.

The only type of corporation was just a "corporation."

It is now referred to as a "C Corporation," even though it is still the same corporation.

And there is still only one type of corporation, the C Corporation.

In a C Corporation, which we will call a C Corp, the income accounting and the payment of taxes are done at the corporate level. The IRS calls this "the entity level."

The after-tax profits of the corporation are used to pay dividends to the shareholders, and the shareholders are taxed again on the same money.

This is the "double taxation" applied to the C Corp.

But there is a provision in the corporate tax laws called "Subchapter S" which allows owners of a C Corp to elect to be treated as an S Corporation, which we will call an S Corp.

In an S Corp, the income is not taxed at the corporate level.

All of the income, credits, and deductions pass through to the Shareholders.

That's why an S Corp is called a "Pass-Through Entity" (PTE).

In order for a C Corp to become an S Corp, all of the Shareholders must sign and file Form 2553, Election by a Small Business Corporation.

The S Corp will file an annual tax return on Form 1120S, which identifies the income, credits, and deductions, and assigns those to the Shareholders in proportion to their ownership percentages.

The Shareholders receive a Schedule K-1 (1120S) and will report the income, credits, and deductions that are allocated to them on their personal tax return.

FORMATION

There is no "formation" for an S Corp.

You become an S Corp by first being a Limited Liability Company (LLC) or a C Corporation.

Let's look at the C Corp situation first.

What you do is create a C Corp and then file Form 2553 Election by a Small Business Corporation in which you elect to be treated as an S Corp for tax purposes.

Treatment as an S Corp means that all of the income, deductions, and credits will pass through to you instead of being taxed at the corporate level.

An S Corp can only have a single class of stock, can have only up to 100 Shareholders, can only have U.S. residents as Shareholders, and the Shareholders cannot be an LLC, C Corp, or Limited Partnership.

Many "tax experts" say that you should not elect Sub S status right away, and see what your levels of income and activity are first.

The Form 2553 Instructions require you to file your election within 75 days of your incorporation or within two months and 15 days after the beginning of the tax year in which the election is to become effective.

But these "experts" say that you can "retroactively elect Sub S status" and "retroactively reclassify distributions as salary."

NO, you cannot.

First, your accounting software can't handle it.

Second, it is against the rules.

Third, if you are ever examined and the Tax Examiner tracks your entries and sees that you have altered the accounting, he can write you up, and he can refer you to the Justice Department for investigation for Tax Fraud. He probably won't, but HE CAN. Are you comfortable with that?

Don't do it.

Make your election within the required time period, and don't try to play games.

The second route to becoming an S Corp is to first create an LLC.

Then you file the Form 2553, just like you do with a C Corp, and you elect to have the LLC treated for tax purposes as an S Corp.

All of the other rules are the same.

You file Form 1120S U.S. Income Tax for an S Corporation, and send a Schedule K-1 (1120S) to each owner of the LLC or the C Corp.

FINANCING

The financing of an S Corp is the same as for a C Corp, if that is where you started, and for an LLC, if you took that route.

MANAGEMENT

An S Corp that started as a C Corp is managed the same way as a C Corp.

An S Corp that started as an LLC is managed the same way that an LLC is managed.

The "S Corp" is not a type of Entity, it is a "tax election."

The underlying Entity is still there, governed by its own formation documents and State law.

OPERATING THE BUSINESS

If the S Corp started as a C Corp, the business is operated the same way as a C Corp is operated.

If the S Corp started as an LLC, the business is operated the same way that an LLC is operated.

BUYING REAL ESTATE

If the S Corp started as a C Corp, then real estate is purchased the same way that it is purchased by a C Corp.

If the S Corp started as an LLC, then the real estate is purchased the same way that it is purchased by an LLC.

CONTRIBUTING OWNED REAL ESTATE

If the S Corp started as a C Corp, then contributing owned real estate to an S Corp in exchange for shares will usually be a taxable transaction.

However, it will not be considered a taxable event if, after the transfer:

1.) the transferor owns at least 80% of the shares authorized to vote, and

2.) the transferor only receives share of stock, and not cash.

If the S Corp started as an LLC, then contributing owned real estate in return for a Capital Interest in the LLC is not a taxable transaction at the time of transfer.

However, there are many reasons for not contributing owned real estate to an entity in return for equity, and you should read the Section on "Contributing Owned Real Estate" in Chapter 2 Limited Liability Company to understand all of the problems you would be creating.

SELLING REAL ESTATE

If the S Corp started as a C Corp, the selling of real estate should be done the same way as with a C Corp.

If the S Corp started as an LLC, the selling of real estate should be done the same way as it is with an LLC.

PROVIDING SERVICES

If your S Corp started as a C Corp, providing services to your S Corp is one of the major differences from operating with a C Corp.

The income from your S Corp will not be taxed at the corporate level.

Instead, it will pass through to you and be taxed at your personal income tax rate.

But, the income will not be considered self-employment income, and therefore will not be subject to the Social Security tax and the Medicare tax.

And that is why, if you perform any services for the S Corp, you must have the S Corp pay you a salary for those services, and the salary must be a reasonable amount.

A salary of $45,000 that the S Corp pays you will be deductible by the corporation as an expense, along with one-half of the 15.3% Self-Employment Tax that the corporation must send to the IRS.

The other one-half of the 15.3% will be withheld from your paycheck.

After the S Corp calculates all of its income, and deducts all of its expenses, including your wages and the matching portion of the Social Security and Medicare Tax, the S Corp will file Form 1120S as its annual tax return, but will pay no taxes.

Along with the tax return, the S Corp will prepare a Schedule K-1 (1120S) and pass through to you the appropriate share of income, deductions, credits and other items, which you will report on your personal tax return, and it will not be considered Self-Employment income, and not subject to the 12.8% Social Security Tax.

If your S Corp started as an LLC, you will be subject to the same rules, and will receive the same documents.

BOOKKEEPING

If you started with a C Corp, the bookkeeping is the same as it would be for a C Corp, except that the Basis of each Shareholder in their stock must be tracked in a separate account, because there is a limit on the amount of losses that can be passed through.

If you started with an LLC, the bookkeeping will be the same as it would for an LLC, in which you are already tracking the Capital Interest of the Members.

If you have employees, or even if you are just paying yourself a salary, it is probably a good idea to have an arrangement with a Bookkeeping Service to handle your Bookkeeping and your Payroll.

It is a good idea to learn it yourself, so that you are a better Business Manager, but then free up your time by turning it over to someone that can do it and meet with you on a regular basis and discuss it.

LIABILITY

If you started as a C Corp, the Shareholders of an S Corp are shielded from any personal liability because it is the same as a C Corp. It is a separate legal entity from the owners.

If you started as an LLC, review the Liability section of Chapter 2 Limited Liability Company. Having elected S Corp status does not change your liability profile.

ENTITY

If you started as a C Corp, the S Corp is a still a separate legal entity, liable for all corporate activities.

If you started as an LLC, the S Corp status does not alter the liability of the LLC as an Entity.

INDIVIDUAL

If you started as a C Corp, the individual Shareholder is still not part of the S Corp, and is not subject to any personal liability arising from the operation of the corporation.

If you started as an LLC, electing S Corp tax status does not alter your liability profile.

TAXATION

This is the major difference between a C Corp and an S Corp.

The income of an S Corp is not taxed at the corporate level, but passes through to the individual Shareholders and is reported on their individual tax returns.

The same is true if you are an LLC that has elected S Corp tax status. The Members will receive the income, deduction, credits and other items on a Schedule K-1 (1120S) to report on their personal tax returns.

FEDERAL

The S Corp will file a Form 1120S U.S. Income Tax Return for an S Corporation, regardless of whether it is a C Corp with S Corp tax status, or an LLC with S Corp tax status.

ENTITY

All of the S Corp's business activities are reported on Form 1120S.

The return includes a Schedule K-1(Form 1120S) which assigns the income, deductions, and credits to the individual Shareholder(s) of the C Corp, and the Members of the LLC.

The income, deductions, and credits are passed through to the individual taxpayers and are reported and taxed at the individual level.

The Shareholders and Members transfer the numbers from the Schedule K-1 to the Form 1040 U.S. Individual Income Tax Return, and attaches the Schedule K-1 to the return when it is sent in.

INDIVIDUAL

Income from the S Corp is passed through to the individual Shareholder or Member, and taxes are assessed at the personal level.

The income qualifies for the Section 199A 20% Qualified Business Income Exclusion because both the C Corp/S Corp and the LLC/S Corp have chosen to be taxed as a Pass-Through Entity (PTE).

The income is not considered Self-Employment (SE) income, so it is not subject to the 15.3% SE Tax.

The IRS does require that the S Corp pay the Shareholder or Member what the IRS considers a "reasonable salary," and that term is defined based on the type of business and the role of the individual.

This is very important if you do not have other W-2 income of at least $128,700 (2018), which would mean that you have paid the maximum amount of Social Security Tax for which a single Taxpayer is liable.

If you have already paid the maximum amount (or had it withheld, actually), then you would only be liable for the Medicare portion of the 15.3% SE Tax, which would be 2.9%.

If both you and your Spouse own the S Corp, you can decide whether to pay a "reasonable salary" to both of you. You do not have to do so if you state that your spouse does not "materially participate" in operating the business.

STATE

There are seven States which have no State Income Tax.

They are:

1.) Alaska,

2.) Florida,

3.) Nevada,

4.) South Dakota,

5.) Texas,

6.) Washington, and

7.) Wyoming.

The other States impose some type of tax on income.

The tax rates vary, and the exceptions, exemptions, and thresholds vary.

ENTITY

If the S Corp is domiciled in, or is doing business in, a State that has an income tax, then that State may or may not adhere to the same rules as the IRS regarding the income being passed through to the Shareholder.

If the State does not have the same rules, the S Corp might have to report the income the same as a C Corp, and pay taxes at the corporate level.

Fortunately, most States follow the IRS model, and just require the filing of an information form and the allow the pass through of the income, deductions, and credits.

INDIVIDUAL

If your State has an income tax, you will need to follow the rules regarding the reporting of S Corp income and the payment of taxes.

CONCLUSION

The S Corp, out of a C Corp or an LLC, is normally not the first choice for operating a rental real estate business.

The LLC is the most used format, either choosing to be taxed as a Disregarded Entity for a Single Member or as a Partnership for a Multi Member LLC.

But for an operating business, the S Corp in the overwhelming choice for a C Corp, and is the second most-used platform for the LLC.

For the C Corp, the primary advantage of the S Corp Election is to become a Pass-Through Entity (PTE), and avoid the 21% tax at the corporate level. A secondary advantage is to receive the 20% Income Exclusion of Section 199A available for PTEs.

And it doesn't hurt that the income of an S Corp, as it drops through to the individual Shareholders, is considered by the IRS to <u>not</u> be self-employment income, so it avoids the 15.3% Self-Employment (SE) Tax.

For the LLC that is not a rental real estate company and chooses S Corp status, it allows the owners to avoid a large portion of the SE Tax that would be assessed on their business if they operated it as a Disregarded Entity or Partnership, and received the business income.

For both the C Corp/S Corp and the LLC/S Corp, the requirements of maintaining S Corp status mean that all of the income of the company cannot drop through to the owners as exempt from SE Tax, because this is obviously a self-employment activity.

So, the S Corp is required to pay the owners a "reasonable salary" which, in some cases, can be as low as 30-35% of the net income.

But that means that the rest of the income can be distributed to the owners as profit, and be exempt from SE Tax.

Like the C Corp/S Corp, this is the major attraction for the LLC/S Corp.

So, for both the C Corp and the LLC, the S Corp tax election is usually the right move to make.

CHAPTER 5

GENERAL PARTNERSHIP

OVERVIEW

A General Partnership is like a Sole Proprietorship, except that it involves more than one person.

A General Partnership is automatically created when two or more persons start a business.

We will refer to "two" so as to keep it simple.

But there will be no systemic differences between two and more than two.

A General Partnership can also be an association of two legal entities that are not individuals.

For Example, two LLCs can enter into a General Partnership arrangement.

If they do, this will create a stacked entity arrangement in which the main activity is being conducted as a Partnership, and then the Partners are operating as a different entity.

For Example, one of the LLCs can be a Single Member LLC that has elected to be treated as a Disregarded Entity for tax purposes, and the other LLC can be a Single Member LLC that has elected to be treated as an S Corp for tax purposes.

Or, the second LLC can be a Multi Member LLC that has elected to be treated as a Partnership for tax purposes.

The General Partnership arrangement can be just the final way in which the Entities have decided to set things up.

So, the general warning that you should never operate as a General Partnership is not always correct.

FORMATION

There is no formality, or legal procedure, required to form a General Partnership.

It can be done just by two persons starting a business, or investing in property.

However, this is a very, very bad way to do it.

The majority of business disputes that I have seen in the past forty years involved two persons who suddenly claimed to have different understandings concerning their business arrangement.

The correct way to form a General Partnership is to create a General Partnership Agreement.

The Agreement will state the terms of the business arrangement and how the Partnership will be formed, operated, and dissolved.

MICHAEL LANTRIP

It will cover such matters as:

1.) Initial Capital Contribution.
2.) Ownership Percentage.
3.) Profit and Loss Allocation.
4.) Division of tasks and responsibilities.
5.) Management.
6.) Dispute resolution.
7.) Dissolution and distribution of assets.

You might be required to file or register your Partnership with the State, depending on where you live.

You will also need to file an Assumed Name Certificate, or whatever is required in the jurisdiction in which you live.

Your Partnership must have a name, such as ABC Partnership.

The Assumed Name Certificate which you file in the county records will identify the Partnership, the Partners, and the address of the business.

And finally, you will need to obtain an Employer Identification Number (EIN) from the IRS.

FINANCING

A General Partnership is a legal entity and can enter into a loan agreement with a Lender in order to obtain financing.

The debt will be secured by the assets of the General Partnership, and the Lender will probably require an additional Guarantee from such of the Partners who have the credit to satisfy the Lender.

The ownership of the General Partnership will generally follow the amount of the capital contributions.

If Bob puts in $100,000 and John and Mary each put in $50,000, then Bob will own 50% of the General Partnership, and John and Mary will each own 25%.

The Partners are also allowed to contribute property in return for ownership interest in the General Partnership.

This will not usually be a taxable event, but it will require careful accounting of the Partners Capital Accounts to make sure that all rules of the IRS are followed.

Contributing property with debt is particularly tricky and will require some complicated calculations by an accountant.

MANAGEMENT

If there is no written agreement, a General Partnership is managed by all of the Partners.

If there is a written agreement, the management will be stipulated in the written agreement.

If there are more than a few Partners, of if most of the Partners do not have the time to take part, the written agreement will designate one person as the Managing Partner.

The IRS will require a declaration of who will be the Tax Partner, a very important position. The Tax Partner deals with the IRS on behalf of the Partnership.

For the person agreeing to be the Tax Partner, it entails a lot of responsibility, and some liability.

For the rest of the Partners, it could mean turning over the right to make decisions affecting the General Partnership and the other Partners without consultation, and without recourse.

Be very careful with the Tax Partner designation.

OPERATING THE BUSINESS

A written partnership agreement will stipulate the manner in which the General Partnership will be managed.

You are free to write the Partnership Agreement to include any provisions that you like, but you should be aware that the general public is entitled to accept the statements and behavior of any Partner as representing the entire General Partnership, and any Partner can create binding obligations and liability.

The actions of any Partner that result in a claim or lawsuit can also cause those actions to be taken against the General Partnership.

It is critical to have very strict control measures in place for a General Partnership.

BUYING REAL ESTATE

The real estate can be purchased in the name of the General Partnership, but if there is no written agreement that outlines the terms of the purchase, management, and eventual sale of the property, it can lead to the real estate being locked into a contested ownership situation and might cause the real estate to become unmarketable.

It is usually best to own the real estate in the name of the General Partnership, but it is critical that this subject be thoroughly detailed in the Partnership Agreement.

And if Partners are required by the Lender to stand behind any financing, it is always better for the Guaranty used to be one in which the Partners are only responsible for any loss the Lender may suffer if it becomes necessary to foreclose on the real estate and sell it to recover the loan proceeds.

The other Guaranty is one where the Partners become immediately responsible if the Lender sends a notice of default or delinquency, and this should be avoided if possible.

CONTRIBUTING OWNED REAL ESTATE

Contributing real estate to a General Partnership in return for Partnership Interest is a possible way of funding the enterprise.

But the possible complications are too numerous to go into here, and would require discussing your particular situation with an accountant who is very knowledgeable about partnership accounting.

And there are many other ways of arriving at the same situation without this complication.

As an Example, you might create an LLC and contribute your real estate to the Single Member LLC in return for all of the Capital Interest. And then your LLC can lease the real estate to the General Partnership, and the General Partnership will function basically as an operating company with limited ownership of assets.

SELLING REAL ESTATE

If the real estate is owned by the General Partnership, then the General Partnership will be the Seller of the real estate.

It will be done in the manner provided for in the Partnership Agreement.

Selling the real estate just has the effect of turning one Partnership asset, real estate, into another Partnership asset, cash.

So the Net Sales Proceeds of the transaction will be owned by the Partners in the same proportion that the real estate was owned by the General Partnership.

The profit from the sale will be Capital Gains, and will be reported to the Partners on their individual Schedule K-1 (1065) from the annual tax return filed by the General Partnership, the Form 1065.

Part of the Capital Gains will be taxed at a different rate, 25%, because it will represent Depreciation Recapture for the depreciation taken on the property while it was being used as rental real estate.

PROVIDING SERVICES

If the General Partnership is engaged in rental real estate activities, the income created will be passive income.

There will be no Self-Employment (SE) Tax assessed on it, so you do not have to be concerned about dealing with how you provide services to the Partnership.

If you run the rental activities, your compensation will be the income earned by the business.

You can provide as much, or as little, personal service as you wish.

It will not make the income self-employment income, and you will not have to pay the 15.3% SE tax.

That's the good news.

The bad news is that it will still be passive income, and any losses cannot be deducted from your other ordinary income, only from other passive income.

BOOKKEEPING

Partnership Accounting is a special area of Accounting, and is also one of the more difficult areas of Accounting.

Not only must you keep track of the Income and Expenses of the Partnership, but you must also keep track of each Partner's Distributive Share Items.

These include:

1.) Income/Loss.

2.) Deductions.

3.) Self-Employment Earnings.

4.) Credits.

5.) Foreign Transactions.

6.) Alternative Minimum Tax (AMT) Items.

7.) Other Information, such as investment income, tax-exempt interest, etc.

Then you must keep track of each Partner's Capital Account.

The cost of Accounting, and the cost of preparing Tax Returns and Schedules for the Partnership and for the Partners are two of the reasons for not choosing the Partnership as your business entity.

On the other hand, there are so many things you can do with the Partnership business entity structure, it offers more opportunities some of the others.

LIABILITY

A General Partnership has no limit on liability.

All of its assets are subject to the debts of the Partnership.

In addition, each Partner has unlimited liability for all of the Partnership obligations.

If that Partner is an individual, then that liability can spread to all of the individual's personal assets, and even business assets if they are not protected inside a Business Entity.

If the Partner is an LLC, the LLC still has unlimited liability for all of the Partnership obligations, but that liability does not extend to the Owner or Owners of the LLC, who are protected from the liabilities of the LLC.

ENTITY

The General Partnership is a legal entity and can be sued in its own capacity.

The General Partnership has unlimited liability for all of its own activities, and in most cases, the activities of the individual Partners if those activities are associated with the General Partnership.

INDIVIDUAL

For the individual, it is one step farther than when you are a Sole Proprietor and responsible for the debts you create in your company.

In the General Partnership, you are also responsible for debts created by another Partner.

In addition, if the actions of another Partner result in a lawsuit that leads to a Judgment against the General Partnership, you are also responsible for that, even if you did not know about it.

This is because each Partner is an agent of the General Partnership with full authority to bind the General Partnership, and thereby, bind the other Partners, provided that the Partner was acting within the scope of the General Partnership's normal business.

TAXATION

A General Partnership does not pay federal income taxes.

But the Partners do.

So, the General Partnership must file a federal income tax form that shows the IRS the amount of income, expenses, deductions, credits, and other items, for both the Partnership and for the Partners.

It is a Form 1065, U.S. Return of Partnership Income.

The General Partnership is a Pass-Through Entity (PTE), so all of the income, deductions, credits, and other items will pass through to the Partners.

In the States that have an income tax, the form for reporting the State income will be whatever your State requires.

FEDERAL

The required tax form for paying federal taxes is the Form 1065, U.S. Return of Partnership Income.

But the General Partnership does not pay taxes.

So, the Form 1065 will report the income, expenses, deductions and credits.

Form 1065 contains a schedule called Schedule K.

Schedule K will identify the different types of income, and any credits and deductions that are not deductible at the Partnership level.

The preparer of the Form 1065 will also prepare a Schedule K-1 for each of the Partners, based on the Schedule K.

The Schedule K-1 will allocate the appropriate amounts of income, credits and deductions for each of the Partners.

A copy of the Form 1065, including Schedule K, and all of the K-1s, is sent to the IRS.

Partners will receive a copy of their K-1 for use in preparing their personal tax returns.

You can obtain a copy for the Form 1065 at:

Irs.gov/pub/irs-pdf/f1065.pdf.

You can obtain a copy of the Schedule K-1 at:

Irs.gov/pub/irs-pdf/f1065sk1.pdf.

ENTITY

The reason that the General Partnership does not pay taxes is because it is what is referred to as a "Pass-Through Entity," or PTE.

That means that all of the income, credits and deductions are passed through to the Partners, who report the appropriate amounts on their personal tax returns.

The new 20% Income Exclusion for Qualified Business Income (QBI) of Pass-Through Entities is not deducted at the Partnership level.

Only the individual Taxpayer can claim this exclusion, and the exclusion will be calculated based on the total of that individual's PTE income.

INDIVIDUAL

The individual Taxpayer, the Partner, will receive a Schedule K-1 that contains information about the Partnership and information about the Partner.

When you receive your Schedule K-1 (Form 1065) it will contain all of the information regarding your share of the Partnership's income/loss, deductions, credits, and other items.

It will include amounts for:

1.) Ordinary business income/loss.

2.) Net rental real estate income/loss.

3.) Other net rental income/loss.

4.) Guaranteed payments.

5.) Interest income.

6a.) Ordinary dividends.

6b.) Qualified dividends.

7.) Royalties.

8.) Net short-term capital gains/loss.

9a.) Net long-term capital gains/loss.

9b.) Collectibles (28%) gains/loss.

9c.) Depreciation Recapture.

10.) Net business asset sale gain/loss.

11.) Other income/loss.

12.) Section 179 deduction.

13.) Other deductions.

14.) Self-employment earnings/loss.

15.) Credits.

16.) Foreign transactions.

17.) Alternative Minimum Tax (AMT) items.

18.) Tax-exempt income and nondeductible expenses.

19.) Distributions.

20.) Other information.

Included with the Schedule K-1 will be extensive directions on exactly where you should put each of the numbers from the K-1 onto your personal tax return.

You will be taxed on these items whether or not you receive the income from the Partnership in the form of a distribution.

The income is added to your Partner Capital Account, and the distributions to you are subtracted from your Partner Capital Account. The balance in your Partner Capital Account is called you "tax basis."

As long as you report your K-1 income on your personal tax return, and as long as your Partner Capital Account balance does not go negative, your distributions themselves are not taxable.

STATE

There are seven States which have no State Income Tax.

They are:

1.) Alaska,

2.) Florida,

3.) Nevada,

4.) South Dakota,

5.) Texas,

6.) Washington, and

7.) Wyoming.

The other States impose some type of tax on income.

The tax rates vary, and the exceptions, exemptions, and thresholds vary.

ENTITY

To determine how your State treats General Partnership, you should access your State's website and read about taxation of Entities.

The situation is different for every State.

INDIVIDUAL

To determine how your State treats Schedule K-1 items, you should access your State's website and read about taxation.

The situation is different for every State.

CONCLUSION

General Partnerships, with individuals as the Partners, are almost never a good idea.

However, the General Partnership is a clean and simple way to structure some businesses, if you take the precautions to limit the liability of each of the participants.

It is not unusual for a General Partnership to be formed by a couple of LLCs.

One reason for this would be that the LLCs already have their own liability, but limit the liability for the Owners, and so the unlimited liability of the General Partnership is not a concern.

Another reason would be that one of the two individuals creating the LLCs wants to be taxed as a Disregarded Entity and the other individual creating the other LLC wants to be taxed as an S Corp.

If they just created a Multi Member LLC, they would both be relegated to Partnership as a default taxation, and if they elected a different one, it would have to be the same for both.

But in most situations, two LLCs would not form a General Partnership.

Given the circumstances, the two individuals would each form their own LLC so that they could each choose their own form of taxation, and then the two LLC would create another LLC together instead of joining into a General Partnership arrangement.

General Partnerships have their uses, but with the flexibility of the LLC, and the special tax features of the S Corp, the General Partnership is not very popular anymore.

CHAPTER 6

LIMITED PARTNERSHIP

OVERVIEW

A Limited Partnership is a partnership made up of a General Partner and one or more Limited Partners.

The General Partner is the Manager, and bears all of the liability for the Limited Partnership.

The General Partner does not have to be an individual, but can be a C Corp, S Corp, or Limited Liability Company (LLC).

The Limited Partners have no liability for the operation of the Limited Partnership beyond the amount of their initial investment.

The Limited Partners are prohibited from taking part in the operation or decision-making of the management of the Limited Partnership.

There are no shares of stock. Ownership is represented by units called Partnership Interests.

The formation is accomplished by filing a Certificate of Limited Partnership with the Secretary of State of the State where the Limited Partnership is domiciled.

The agreement, or contract, between and among the participants is the Limited Partnership Agreement.

Like the LLC, the S Corp, and the General Partnership, the Limited Partnership is a Pass-Through Entity (PTE).

FORMATION

The Limited Partnership (LP) is created by the filing of a Certificate of Limited Partnership with the State in which the Limited Partnership is domiciled.

It varies from State to State, but information required in a Certificate of Limited Partnership might include:

1.) Name of the Limited Partnership.

2.) Name and addresses of all General Partners.

3.) Number of General Partners required to amend the Certificate.

4.) Name and address of the Registered Agent.

5.) Term or duration of the Limited Partnership.

6.) A brief description of the character or purpose of the business.

7.) Location of the principal place of business.

8.) Names and resident addresses of all Limited Partners.

9.) Amount of cash contributed by each Limited Partner.

10.) Description of any other property, and its agreed value, contributed by each Limited Partner.

11.) Additional future contributions that must be make by Limited Partners, including the timing and conditions.

12.) Details of any agreements to return the investments of the Limited Partners.

13.) Details of profit-sharing, payments, or other methods of compensating the Limited Partners.

14.) Conditions regarding the transfer of Limited Partnership interest.

15.) Rights of the General Partner to admit new Limited Partners.

16.) How profits are distributed, and the priority.

Some States have a mandatory Form that must be used.

Then, another document, called a Limited Partnership Agreement, is signed by the General Partner and the Limited Partners.

All States have Partnership statutes that control what a LP can and cannot do. But many of these matters can be overridden with a provision in the Limited Partnership Agreement.

The Limited Partnership Agreement can be used to prevent outside ownership, or prevent an unwanted spouse from inheriting the Partnership interest, with use of Right of First Refusal provisions.

And the Limited Partnership Agreement generally outlines the interests of the Limited Partners.

Limited Partnership interests are also classified as securities. So, depending on who you are selling to, and how you are doing the selling, you might be required to comply with State and Federal securities laws.

Limited Partnerships do not have perpetual life.

They can, and will, be terminated under certain conditions.

1.) The Limited Partnership can expire under the terms and conditions set forth in the Certificate of Limited Partnership.

2.) The Limited Partnership can expire by unanimous agreement of all members, General Partner and all Limited Partners.

3.) The Limited Partnership can end with a change in any of the basic elements described in the Certificate of Limited Partnership, requiring the filing of a new Certificate of Limited Partnership.

4.) The Limited Partnership can be dissolved by the Court in any matter that has resulted in the filing of a lawsuit and rendering of a verdict requiring dissolution.

FINANCING

The Limited Partnership is essentially a vehicle for raising capital.

The General Partner sells Limited Partnership interests to investors to get funds that are used to purchase the assets for the Limited Partnership.

It is like a corporation selling stock, but much easier, and does not involve the manager giving up control of the operation because Limited Partners are prohibited from taking part in the management or operation of the business.

The investors might be offered a guaranteed annual return regardless of profitability, or a guaranteed cut of annual profit, or a guaranteed annual percentage of their investment returned, or anything that will induce them to purchase the Limited Partnership interests.

Usually the Partners contribute cash, all at once, and at nearly the same time, because this is what is required by the General Partner.

But almost any other arrangement is possible, such as an initial set amount, and then regular periodic contributions of set amounts. This would involve the use of a Promissory Note.

Some Limited Partnership Agreements provide for a "cash call" in the event of financial problems, but most General Partners find it difficult to get the Limited Partners to agree to such terms.

Limited Partnership interests are usually transferable to a third party, and some State laws require that they be freely transferrable, but this does not entail transfer of any ownership of interest in the real estate owned by the Limited Partnership, only the transfer of the interest owned in the Limited Partnership.

But usually the General Partner wants to place restrictions on the transfer of interests, and this is allowed by law.

The restrictions might include the requirement that a transferee be approved by the other Partners, or that the new Partner only receive financial benefits, such as distribution of profits, and not receive voting rights or other rights of ownership.

MANAGEMENT

The unique feature of the Limited Partnership is that the Limited Partners have nothing to do with the management of the Entity.

If fact, they are prohibited from taking part.

If they do, they lose their limit on their liability.

This can sometimes lead to an agonizing situation where the Limited Partnership is in financial trouble, the General Partner either is not, or cannot, do anything about it, and the Limited Partners must stand by and watch, because they are prohibited from getting involved.

The Limited Partnership is managed solely by the General Partner.

OPERATING THE BUSINESS

The General Partner will operate the Limited Partnership in any way that he chooses.

It is in his best interest to operate it effectively and profitably because his best interest is usually served by a growing, successful, and profitable company.

The General Partner will make all of the decisions that he is permitted to make under the terms of the Limited Partnership Agreement.

The operating funds of the Limited Partnership will usually be a portion of the funds received from the Limited Partners in return for their interests in the Limited Partnership.

If there are situations that the Limited Partners are permitted to vote on, the General Partner will call a meeting to handle the matter.

Even though Annual Meetings are not usually required by law, the General Partner will usually have an Annual Meeting. And in order to maintain good relations with the Limited Partners, he will have at least Quarterly Meetings. And, depending on the nature of the business, it will not be unusual to have Monthly Meetings to keep the Limited Partners aware of everything that is going on.

BUYING REAL ESTATE

The Limited Partnership is an Entity which is primarily used to raise funds for investment, and the funds are most often used to buy investment real estate.

The real estate will be purchased in the name of the Limited Partnership.

The real estate will be owned by the Limited Partnership.

Neither the General Partner nor the Limited Partners will own an interest in the real estate.

Part of the funds that the Limited Partnership receives from selling interests in the Limited Partnership to the Limited Partners will be used as a Down Payment for purchasing the real estate, and the remainder of the purchase price will be borrowed.

The Limited Partners will have no liability for repayment of the loan.

The General Partner, and the Limited Partnership, will be responsibility for the repayment of the loan.

CONTRIBUTING OWNED REAL ESTATE

Contributing real estate to a Limited Partnership in return for Partnership Interest is legal and is sometimes done.

But the possible complications are too numerous to go into here, and would require discussing your particular situation with an accountant who is very knowledgeable about partnership accounting.

However, there are many reasons for not contributing owned real estate to an entity in return for equity, and you should read the Section on "Contributing Owned Real Estate" in Chapter 2 Limited Liability Company to understand all of the problems you could be creating.

SELLING REAL ESTATE

The real estate is being held in the name of the Limited Partnership, and the Limited Partnership will be the Seller of the real estate.

Often, a Limited Partnership created for the purpose of investing in real estate will have an ultimate plan of selling the real estate.

The General Partner will sign the deed on behalf of the Limited Partnership.

But whether he can make this decision to sell without consultation with the Limited Partners, or without their consent, majority or unanimous, will depend on the terms set out in the Limited Partnership Agreement.

Often, a real estate Limited Partnership will have as part of its business plan to engage in a Section 1031 Like Kind Exchange and use the Net Sales Proceeds from the sale of the real estate to purchase another property and thereby avoid payment of the Capital Gains tax and the Depreciation Recapture tax.

If this is part of the plan, it must be laid out in the Limited Partnership Agreement, and it must stipulate whether the Limited Partners must all consent to doing a Section 1031 Exchange when the time comes, or whether they consent at the time of signing the Limited Partnership Agreement. Some Limited Partners might not want to be locked in for the period of time it would take to go through two investments.

If no Section 1031 Exchange occurs, the sale will be reported by the Limited Partnership, and the income, deductions, credits and other items will be reported on the individual K-1s of the Limited Partners.

The amount of Capital Gains tax liability and Depreciation Recapture tax liability will depend on the specific tax profile of the Limited Partner.

If the real estate is sold, it will probably mean the winding up of the Limited Partnership, since it no longer has any assets.

This will be covered in the Limited Partnership Agreement.

PROVIDING SERVICES

If you are the General Partner of a Limited Partnership, you will be providing your personal services to the Limited Partnership. That's what a General Partner does, manage the Limited Partnership.

The General Partner benefits financially in a number of ways in a Limited Partnership.

The General Partner will usually receive a fee for setting up the Limited Partnership. This will be a percentage of the total value of the business, just like a Limited Partner interest.

The General Partner will usually receive a fee for arranging the financing of the Limited Partnership. This will also be a percentage.

The General Partner will usually receive a Management Fee. This will usually be in the form of monthly payments, coming from operating reserve or from cash flow.

So, when the Limited Partnership is up and running, the General Partner will own a percentage of the enterprise, like the Limited Partners, and will also be receiving a monthly fee similar to wages for managing the Limited Partnership.

On the other hand, Limited Partners are prohibited from providing personal services to the Limited Partnership because that is an act which could cause them to lose their status as a Limited Partner, and subject them to the same liability as the General Partner.

BOOKKEEPING

Bookkeeping for a Limited Partnership is done on two levels.

There will be regular bookkeeping of the business, just like there would be with any other business, keeping tract of income, expenses, depreciation, monthly or quarterly government reports, withholding Social Security and Medicare amounts from employee wages and sending to the IRS, and preparing monthly Income Statements and Balance Sheets.

Then there will be the bookkeeping required by the terms of the Limited Partnership Agreement.

This will keep tract of such things as Partners Capital Accounts, income allocations, guaranteed payments, percentage payouts, return of investments, and all of the other matters that affect the Limited Partners' investments and the Limited Partnerships obligations to the Limited Partners as stipulated by the Limited Partnership Agreement.

LIABILITY

All of the liability of a Limited Partnership is borne by the General Partner.

ENTITY

If the Limited Partnership is sued, the General Partner will be sued as well.

If a Judgment is obtained against the Limited Partnership, the assets of the Limited Partnership can be taken and sold to satisfy the Judgment.

INDIVIDUAL

The Limited Partners have no liability for the operation of the Limited Partnership.

If the Limited Partnership runs out of money, the Limited Partners will only lose what they have invested in purchasing their Limited Partnership interest.

If the Limited Partnership commits an act that causes it to be sued, the Limited Partners will not be parties to the lawsuit. The lawsuit will be against the Limited Partnership and the General Partner.

If a Limited Partner is sued in an unrelated matter and has a Judgment Lien filed against, the Judgment Lien holder cannot take the interest in the Limited Partnership, but can get a Charging Order from the Court directing that any funds received by the Limited Partner from the Limited Partnership, go instead to the Judgment Lien holder.

The same applies if the General Partner is sued in an unrelated matter and has a Judgment Lien filed against him.

See Chapter 18 for a full explanation of Charging Orders.

TAXATION

The Limited Partnership does not pay taxes at the federal level, but must file a tax return, the IRS Form 1065, U.S. Return of Partnership Income, and pass the income, deductions, credits and other items on to the Partners.

FEDERAL

The federal tax form, Form 1065, U.S. Return of Partnership Income is available at:

www.irs.gov/pub/irs-pdf/f1065.pdf

The Instructions are available at:

www.irs.gov/pub/irs-pdf/i1065.pdf

ENTITY

On the Form 1065, the Limited Partnership will provide an accounting of the accounts of the Partners.

It is on the fourth page and it is called Schedule K, Partners' Distributive Share Items.

The first section is called Income, with the following line numbers and items of information.

1. Ordinary business income (loss).

2. Net rental real estate income (loss).

3a. Other gross rental income (loss).

3b. Expenses from other rental activities.

3c. Other net rental income (loss). Subtract 3b from 3a.

4. Guaranteed payments.

5. Interest income.

6a. Ordinary dividends.

6b. Qualified dividends.

6c. Dividend equivalents.

7. Royalties.

8. Net short-term capital gain (loss). Attach Schedule D.

9a. Net long-term capital gain (loss). Attach Schedule D.

9b. Collectibles (28%) gain (loss).

9c. Unrecaptured Section 1250 gain (attach statement).

10. Net Section 1231 gain (loss).

11. Other income (loss) (see instructions).

The second section covers Deductions, and includes things like Depreciation and Investment Interest Expense.

The third section is Self-Employment Income.

The fourth section is Credits, and covers any credits due from rental real estate activities.

Schedule K cover a complete page and has a lot of useful information on it.

I recommend that you download a copy of Form 1065, and go over it.

You don't have to understand all of it to understand some very useful parts of it.

Work on it a little each year and see where your numbers are going, and pretty soon you will be surprised to actually see how it works.

You may never understand all of it. After 35 years, I still have to look stuff up.

INDIVIDUAL

The Limited Partner's share of income is not Self-Employment (SE) income for the Limited Partners, unless it represents Guaranteed Payments for services rendered to the Limited Partnership (LP).

The General Partner's Guaranteed Payments will be SE income.

And the General Partner's share of partnership income will also be SE income unless it is rental income from real estate held for investment, in which case it is considered passive income, and not subject to SE taxation.

STATE

There are seven States which have no State Income Tax.

They are:

1.) Alaska,

2.) Florida,

3.) Nevada,

4.) South Dakota,

5.) Texas,

6.) Washington, and

7.) Wyoming.

The other States impose some type of tax on income.

The tax rates vary, and the exceptions, exemptions, and thresholds vary.

ENTITY

Each State will treat LLC income differently, depending on how you elect to be taxed at the federal level.

Your State website will contain the information you need to deal with this.

INDIVIDUAL

Each State will treat LLC income differently, depending on how you elect to be taxed at the federal level.

Your State website will contain the information you need to deal with this.

CONCLUSION

The Limited Partnership is the best Business Entity to fit the situation where one individual wants to operate a large investment project, but needs to have money from investors.

The Limited Partnership allows the individual to be the General Partner and retain control of the entire project, and have the investors placed in the position of Limited Partners, where they not only have no right to participate in management, but are actually prohibited by law from doing so.

The agreement between the General Partner and the Limited Partners, the Limited Partnership Agreement, will contain all of the conditions of the business relationship, and will determine what the General Partner can and cannot do, what the rights of the Limited Partners are, as well as any dispute resolution.

Of course, most of the information that you will find on the internet today about Limited Partnerships is put there by the Promoters of the Limited Partnerships, and explains in glowing detail all of the benefits available to the Limited Partners.

There is very little information about the possible dangers and negative aspects.

So, whether you are considering being the General Partner or being a Limited Partner, I recommend that you look far beyond the information generally available before you commit to anything.

Partnership law, Partnership taxation, and Partnership accounting are very specialized areas of business, and can be very difficult to engage in successfully.

And, finally, I have not covered the Entity known as a Limited Liability Partnership.

It is different from a Limited Partnership.

It is usually a Partnership made up of professionals such as Attorneys or Doctors, in which they practice together, and all take an active part, but each have their liability limited to their own actions, and are protected from liability arising from the actions of the other practitioners.

I have not covered it because the newer and better way of structuring such an arrangement is to have Multi Member LLC (MMLLC) in which each of the Members is another LLC that is the professional practice of the Attorney or Doctor.

This arrangement is not possible under the laws of some States, but is growing in popularity in other States, because of the total flexibility of the MMLLC's Operating Agreement, which permits any terms that can be imagined, unlike the Limited Liability Partnership, which is limited under Partnership law in what can be included.

CHAPTER 7

A CAUTION ABOUT LAND TRUSTS

WHAT IS A TRUST?

Let's start by looking at the legal elements of a Trust.

There are four:

1. Grantor,

2. Trustee,

3. Beneficiary, and

4. Corpus.

1. GRANTOR

The Grantor is also sometimes called the Trustor or Settlor, but we will use the term "Grantor."

The Grantor is the person who creates the Trust. He is the only one involved at this point, and makes all of the decisions and sets all of the terms.

A Trust is usually created with a written document, called a Trust Agreement.

A Trust <u>can</u> be created orally, and would be legal and binding if it were, but it would be virtually impossible to administer. They are seldom created this way.

Another way that a Trust can be created is by being in a situation where the Court has to declare that a Trust exists because of the statements and behavior of an individual, even if the individual did not intend to create a Trust. This is usually the result of a lawsuit. It is called an Involuntary Trust or Imposed Trust.

But the Trust that we are talking about will be created with a written document called a Trust Agreement.

2. TRUSTEE

The Trustee administers the Trust.

The Trustee is named in the Trust Agreement by the Grantor, and the Trustee's powers, duties, and responsibilities are detailed in the document.

The Trustee is "independent." His actions cannot be directed or influenced by the Grantor or anyone else. If the Trustee is not independent, the Trust is invalid under law.

3. BENEFICIARY

The Beneficiary is the person who receives the benefits of the Trust.

There can be more than one Beneficiary.

The Trust Agreement will contain the details of what the Beneficiary will receive, and the terms and conditions under which the benefits will be received.

The Beneficiary has no say in how the Trust is administered.

4. CORPUS

The "corpus" of the Trust means the body of the Trust.

In other words, the corpus is the asset or assets placed in the Trust.

The asset might be an Installment Note with monthly payments being received, or it might be a Duplex with monthly rent payments being received.

So, those are the legal elements of a Trust.

Now, what does it look like?

Paul Smith of Dallas creates the John Smith Trust for the benefit of his son, John, and funds it with a Duplex.

The John Smith Trust Agreement names William Walker as Trustee. The Agreement instructs the Trustee to collect the rents, pay the expenses, maintain the real property, and distribute a stipulated amount to the Beneficiary each month.

The Agreement might also provide for the Trustee to pay the secondary education expenses of the Beneficiary under certain conditions.

The Agreement contains the provisions for how long the Trust will exist, what will happen at the end, and the fees allowed for the Trustee.

Paul Smith has nothing to do with the Trust after he signs the document. He cannot instruct the Trustee, he cannot take back the property. He cannot revoke the Trust. He cannot amend the Trust.

The transfer of the real property will be done with a Warranty Deed from Paul Smith to "William Walker, Trustee of the John Smith Trust, created March 17, 2018" because in Texas a Trust cannot hold title to real estate, only the Trustee can hold title.

The details contained in the Grantee designation after the name tells anyone searching the records, looking at the ownership of the property, that even though this Duplex is in the name of William Walker, it is not his. He is holding it as a Trustee under the terms of a written Trust Agreement called the "John Smith Trust" and to distinguish the Trust from any other by the same name, this is the one created on March 17, 2018.

This is the standard Trust, and it is an Irrevocable Trust, meeting all of the legal requirements of the laws of the jurisdiction.

Now we will wander into the tall weeds that is a "Land Trust."

WHAT IS A LAND TRUST?

The Land Trust that we are talking about is not the Land Trust that is used for holding large tracts of land or sensitive ecosystems in Trust for environmental reasons, often called a Conservation Land Trust.

We are talking about the Land Trust as a Business Model, a platform for holding income-producing real estate or investment real estate.

There is no Federal Land Trust Law. So the activity is governed on a state-by-state basis.

There are ten (10) states that have passed laws providing for the creation of a Land Trust in their individual states:

1. Alabama,

2. Florida,

3. Georgia,

4. Hawaii,

5. Illinois,

6. Indiana,

7. Louisiana,

8. North Dakota,

9. Ohio, and

10. Virginia.

These are called Land Trust States.

The first state to authorize the creation of a Land Trust was Illinois.

You might think it was done out of an abundance of concern for the small real estate investor. Actually, the Land Trust was were created by Chicago politicians who wanted to hide the fact that they were speculating in land.

As a result, the Land Trust in states where it is authorized by statute is usually referred to as an "Illinois-type" Land Trust.

Each of the state statutes are a little different, so, for purposes of discussion, we will deal with the Illinois statute.

LAND TRUST LAW IN TEN STATES

The term "Land Trust" is used to describe an "arrangement" that is not even a "trust" as that term has ever been defined in law prior to the first "Land Trust."

And to add to the confusion, the "arrangement" uses the designations of Settlor, Trustee, Beneficiary, and Corpus, which are elements of a real trust.

1. Settlor – the person who creates the Trust.

2. Trustee – the person who is supposed to manage the Trust, but actually does what he is told by the Beneficiary, and holds title to the real estate. He does not have to be "independent," can be a brother or sister.

3. Beneficiary – the person who receives the benefits of the Trust. It can be anyone, even the Settlor, and can also be a business entity. The Beneficiary runs the Trust, telling the Trustee when to sell or buy, and collects the rents, etc.

4. Corpus – the real property of the Trust.

In a typical Land Trust:

◊ The Settlor creates the Land Trust, naming the Trustee.

◊ The Settlor deeds real estate to the Trustee.

◊ The Settlor names himself as the Beneficiary.

◊ The Settlor, as Beneficiary, runs the Trust and manages the property.

The Trust document is not filed anywhere publicly. It is just put in a desk drawer, assuming that it ever even existed.

The Land Trust is "revocable," which means that it can be revoked by the Settlor one minute after it is created, or a year later, just by tearing up the original Land Trust Agreement and throwing it in the trash, or by writing "revoked" across it, or by "any other act sufficient to evidence the intent to do so."

In fact, there is no real evidence for you to see that a Land Trust exists, ever existed, or still exists in the future.

If it suits him, the Settlor can say that he revoked the Land Trust at some point in the past, true or not, and no one can prove that he didn't.

The only event that occurred is that the Settlor signed a deed for the real estate to another person, identifying that person as a Trustee, and filed the deed in the public records.

I have studied the Land Trust for a number of years.

If there is a serious reason for doing this even in states where it is authorized, I don't see it.

And I have been doing Asset Protection, Tax Planning, Estate Planning, and Wills and Trust for over 35 years.

Now let's look at what the arrangement looks like in states where it is not specifically authorized by statute.

NOT LAW IN THE REMAINING STATES

In the remaining states, those without a statutory Illinois-type Land Trust, there is no such thing as a Land Trust.

Every state has a body of law that governs the creation and operation of a Trust of any kind, regardless of the asset in the Trust. The rules vary somewhat but are similar and can be explained in general terms.

There are two basic types of Trusts, an Irrevocable Trust and a Revocable Trust.

An Irrevocable Trust is the basic, standard Trust that I discussed at the beginning of this Chapter.

The reason that it must be irrevocable is that in order for the Grantor to receive the benefits available from the use of a Trust in Tax Planning, Estate Planning, and Asset Protection Planning, he must be permanently bound to the terms and conditions of the Trust Agreement. He must permanently give up ownership and control of the real property and he must have nothing to do with the administration of the Trust.

Otherwise, the Grantor could just use the Trust to re-direct the income of the real property to the lower-tax-bracket Beneficiary for awhile, then retire, and revoke the Trust to get the real property and income back.

So we have the Irrevocable Trust.

The other type of Trust is the Revocable Trust.

It is not really a Trust at all, based on the definition at the beginning of the Chapter.

The most common type of Revocable Trust is the Living Trust.

It is more accurately called a Revocable Living Trust, and I have complete information on it in the following Chapter.

When a Land Trust is attempted to be created in a state that does not have a specific statute authorizing it, here is what actually happens.

The owner of real property deeds that real property to a person or entity, identifying it as a Trustee for a named Trust.

The property owner writes up a document claiming to create a Land Trust, and names himself as the Beneficiary and giving himself the right to control the real property and the administration of the "Trust."

Both of these actions are prohibited by the laws of the state.

So, what has actually happened?

We'll look at that in the next section.

THE SHELL GAME AND BOGUS CLAIMS

It is easy to analyze and explain something that has a universally agreed-upon set of rules and procedures. Otherwise, it is difficult, and sometimes impossible.

Virtually no one agrees on the aspects of the Land Trust.

So, the only way to bring any clarity to the situation is to take the claims of the supporters of the arrangement, and look more closely.

What follows are statements about a Land Trust made by promoters, followed by the facts and the law.

"You can form a Land Trust in any state just by forming a Trust under the trust laws of that state and calling it a Land Trust."

No, you cannot. A Land Trust is an entity that is specifically created by the law of the state in which it is created. If the state is not one of the ten states that have authorized the creation of a Land Trust in that state, you cannot create a Land Trust in that state. What you are creating is a Revocable Living Trust, and when you transfer real property to the Trustee of that Trust, you are still personally liable for anything that occurs on the property and for any debts on the property. If the property is producing income, you still personally owe the taxes on that income. The IRS does not recognize the existence of a Revocable Trust for tax purposes. All you have done is to screw up the title to the real property by transferring it to an agent for an entity that exists temporarily, or maybe not at all.

"If you attempt to create a Land Trust in a state without a Land Trust statute, it is still valid because it is just considered a legal contract between the Settlor, the Trustee, and the Beneficiary."

It is not a legal contract. The elements of a binding contract are an offer, plus consideration, and then acceptance. None of those elements are present in this arrangement. In addition, a binding contract requires the signatures of all parties, and the only person signing anything here is the Settlor, and maybe the Trustee, who has given no consideration. So it is not a contract and it is not binding anyone. If the Settlor signed in more than one capacity, it still would not be binding because a person cannot enter into a contract with himself. How would he enforce it, sue himself, and get into a fight with himself? Under the legal concept of Doctrine of Merger, if all of the parties are considered to be the same, a Court can merge them into one and declare the document not a contract.

So, it is not a legal contract.

It is a Revocable Living Trust that can be revoked at any time by one party.

"If you live in a state without a Land Trust statute, you just form a Land Trust in one of the ten states where it is authorized, and use it with real estate in your own state."

Duh!

One of the reasons that each state has its own laws is to control the ownership and use of real estate within its borders. If you go to the trouble and expense of doing this, you will have an entity valid in another state which is not valid in your own state, and it has a Trustee who holds title to real estate in your state which you just deeded away. The Land Trust is not valid in your state, so anything that it does under the Land Trust statute of another state is not valid in your state. If it were, there would be no reason for each state to have its own laws.

"The Land Trust provides 'privacy of ownership' because the Land Trust document is not recorded anywhere and so no one would know who the Beneficiary is."

OK. What if I went to the Court House and looked at the deed putting the real estate into the name of the Trustee? What if I looked in the Mortgage or Deed of Trust records to see who is liable for the debt on the property?   What if I went to the office of the Taxing Authority and looked at who was paying the property taxes before the Trustee started paying them?   What if I checked to see whose name the utilities are in?   What if I asked the tenant where he sends the rent check, or who does his plumbing repair, and then ask the plumber who hired him?

It is no longer possible to hide in this society.

"Privacy of ownership is the most important element of asset protection."

Not only is it not the most important, it isn't even an element at all.

If a judgment creditor, or a judgment lien holder wants to find you, you will be found.   But more likely, the lawsuit will just be filed against the Trustee, and then Discovery will be served on the Trustee requiring him to answer questions under oath, and naming the Beneficiary if one exists.   Otherwise the judgment will be filed against the Trustee and the property will be sold to satisfy it.

If you are sued in another matter and you are attempting to hide your status as Beneficiary, the Discovery served on you will require you to list your assets, and you will be responding under oath.

If you are relying on a Land Trust for anonymity, you will be disappointed.

"Any judgment against the Beneficiary will not affect title to the trust property."

Nonsense.

If the Land Trust is actually valid, and the Beneficiary is someone who owns a "beneficial interest" in the Trust, a judgment creditor can foreclose on that interest, step into the shoes of the Beneficiary, and instruct the Trustee to sell the property and give him the money.

If the Land Trust is not valid (the only other possibility), the Court will rule that the Beneficiary is actually the owner of the property and the judgment creditor will be able to foreclose on it.

<u>"The property will be titled under the name of the trust and not under the name of the property owner."</u>

This is my favorite.

An unrecorded, unregistered entity that only exists (maybe) on a piece of paper in somebody's desk drawer cannot own real property. Title to property in a trust is held in the name of the Trustee, because when it comes time to sell the property, who signs the deed? How do you know this person has the right to sell the property? Do you think you could get a Title Policy on the property?

I could go on forever with these, but you see what I am telling you.

CONCLUSION

A Land Trust does not offer Asset Protection.

A Land Trust does not offer any tax advantages.

A Land Trust does not offer anonymity or even privacy.

A Land Trust does not offer anything that you cannot get with a simple business agreement, except possibly avoiding the "Due on Sale" clause in your mortgage.

And a business agreement would be an instrument that would be acceptable to all parties involved, protecting their interests, as well as any outside party that you wish to involve in the situation.

The fact that a Land Trust is revocable at the whim of the person who created it makes it little more than a joke.

Would you really do business involving an investment instrument that can be torn up at any moment?

As I said, for years I have looked at Land Trusts, trying to find a reason for their existence.

And except for the Chicago aldermen who were hiding their real estate scam in the late 1800s, I have not found one.

CHAPTER 8

A CAUTION ABOUT LIVING TRUSTS

OVERVIEW

A Living Trust is not a Trust.

It is a document that you write saying that you are putting property aside for the benefit of someone, and that you are designating another person to manage the arrangement.

A typical situation would be that you have a Duplex netting $1,200 per month and you want to direct that income to a specific person.

You write a document, or fill out a form, called a Living Trust.

Then you put that document into your desk drawer and no one sees it.

The Trust document is never filed in any public record.

The arrangement can be undone by you at any time, just by ceasing to do whatever you are doing. Or you can tear up the document. Or you can write "revoked" across it. Actually, you can just sell the property and keep the net proceeds yourself, and ignore the document.

That's why the correct legal term for a Living Trust is <u>Revocable</u> Living Trust. You can revoke it during your lifetime.

The Revocable Living Trust does not file a federal income tax return because the IRS does not accept it as a legal entity.

The real estate is still your property because the trust is revocable and cannot own property.

If you deed the property to the Trustee, all that you have accomplished is to just screw up the title, temporarily (see the next section).

The income generated by the property is still your personal income because you have not fully and permanently divested yourself of ownership of the property and the IRS will expect the income to be included on your tax return, and will expect the taxes to be paid by you.

For that reason, the Beneficiary to whom you are directing the income cannot include the income on his tax return because he does not own the property, and the income is actually just a gift from you, because you still own the property. You might have a Gift Tax problem, but that is another discussion.

You remain liable for the debt on the property. The lender can foreclose on the property. You can sell the property.

It's like the Revocable Living Trust doesn't even exist.

So, why would anybody want to create one?

See the next section.

HOW TO USE A LIVING TRUST

A Living Trust does not protect your assets.

The property that you put into a Living Trust is still owned by you because the trust is a Revocable Trust, not a true legal business entity created under State law and filed with the State.

The trust laws of every State provide that if the Grantor of a Revocable Trust is sued, the Court can require the Grantor to revoke the trust and make the property subject to the payment of creditor claims.

So, what purpose, if any, does a Revocable Living Trust serve?

Well, actually, it can serve a very important purpose if it is used the way it should be used.

Here's how that works.

You create a Revocable Living Trust.

You, as Grantor, name yourself as the Trustee.

You also name yourself as the Beneficiary.

You put all of your assets into the Revocable Living Trust.

Then, for the rest of your life, you continue to manage your assets just like you did before the creation of the trust, just like you still owned them all personally, because you do.

You pay the property taxes because you still own the property.

You pay the insurance premiums and name yourself as "loss payee" because you still own the property.

You continue to make payments on the mortgage.

You file your annual tax return and pay the taxes on the income from the property in the Trust because you still own the property.

But, here's where the purpose of the Revocable Living Trust comes into play.

You provide in the Trust Agreement that the Revocable Living Trust becomes <u>Irrevocable</u> upon your death.

At that point it becomes a true legal trust that <u>does</u> own the property.

That is critical because it means that the property is not part of your estate and does not have to be passed to your heirs by using a Will and going through the process of Probate.

Incidentally, the Probate process is not as bad as everyone says it is, if you have a good Lawyer, but it is still a pain.

Now, since you are deceased at this point, you obviously cannot be the Trustee or the Beneficiary.

And this is the reason for having a Revocable Living Trust that become Irrevocable upon your death.

In the Trust Agreement, you provide for a Successor Trustee, and you instruct the Trustee to collect all of your assets that you put into the Trust, pay the debts against them, and distribute them to the Beneficiaries in the manner you describe.

You also name the Successor Beneficiaries, the persons who will become the Beneficiaries after you die. They will receive your assets in the manner that you describe in the Trust Agreement.

All of this takes place without any Court filings, or any Court supervision, and without any public notice.

You are able to pass all of your assets to your heirs without having a Will and without going through probate proceedings.

Of course, you will have a Will, just in case you left an asset out of the Living Trust. But it will be what is called a Pourover Will, and it will just say that you intended to place all of your assets in the Living Trust, and if there are any assets that have not been placed in the Trust, you hereby leave those assets to the Living Trust to be distributed as specified therein.

CONCLUSION

Do not try to use a Revocable Living Trust to do anything during your lifetime.

It is not a real Trust, and the existence will be ignored under law.

It will not protect your assets.

The only possible result will be to screw up title to your real estate.

However, if you use it correctly, a Revocable Living Trust can be an excellent tool to avoid Probate, and should be used in those States which make the Probate process into a living nightmare, like California and New York.

But it is not as simple as everyone claims.

Do not use the packages available on the internet or at the seminars.

Find a good Lawyer (and you might look for the Holy Grail while you are at it, the odds are similar), and have the documents drafted to suit your particular situation.

Doing it right in the first place is the best investment you can make.

CHAPTER 9

INDIVIDUAL TAX RATES

NEW TAX LAW

New Tax Brackets don't come along very often.

But they are here, and you need to adjust your entire frame of reference.

I would like to make this more interesting if I could, but it is just one of those things you must learn, because it affects every decision you will make.

Go through it now, and it will be here for you to refer back to when we talk about Sole Proprietorships and Limited Liability Companies.

WHAT IT IS

Each Taxpayer must pay some amount of taxes based on a computed number called Adjusted Gross Income, referred to as AGI.

Some Taxpayers are allowed to report their income, and take their deductions, together with another Taxpayer. This is determined by their Filing Status, or filing category.

There are four filing categories.

◊ Single (S).

◊ Married, Filing Jointly (MFJ).

◊ Married, Filing Separately (MFS).

◊ Head of Household (HH).

Surviving Widows can qualify to file MFJ.

Each Taxpayer then falls into a Tax Bracket, from 10% to 37%.

A Tax Bracket refers to the taxable rate on the last dollar of marginal income.

The appropriate Tax Bracket for a Taxpayer will be determined by the Taxpayer's AGI.

SUMMARY OF THE NEW LAW

For individual Taxpayers, the highest marginal tax rate on ordinary income is reduced from 39.6% to 37%, and all of the other Tax Brackets are adjusted downward, and result in a reduced tax liability for the same level of income.

NEW LAW EXPLAINED

The Tax Cuts And Jobs Act (TCJA) changes both the Tax Brackets and the cutoff amounts, as well as the Tax Rates.

I'll just do <u>Single</u> and <u>MFJ</u> since you are probably in one of these as a Real Estate Investor.

TAX BRACKETS

10% Tax Bracket

Single: $0 – $9,525

MFJ: $0 – $19,050

12% Tax Bracket

Single: $9,526 – $38,700

MFJ: $19,051 – $77,400

22% Tax Bracket

Single: $38,701 – $82,500

MFJ: $77,401 – $165,000

24% Tax Bracket

Single: $82,501 – $157,500

MFJ: $165,001 – $315,000

32% Tax Bracket

Single: $157,501 – $200,000

MFJ: $315,001 – $400,000

35% Tax Bracket

Single: $200,001 – $500,000

MFJ: $400,001 – $600,000

37% Tax Bracket

Single: $500,001 and more

MFJ: $600,001 and more

The Personal Exemption is eliminated, and the Standard Deduction is increased.

The new Standard Deduction is $12,000 for Singles, $24,000 for MFJs, and $18,000 for a Head of Household.

Now that we have that out of the way, let's look at Corporate Tax Rates, and then move on to the money topics.

CHAPTER 10

CORPORATE TAX RATE

NEW TAX LAW

You will probably not be subject to the Corporate Tax Rate, because you will probably not be operating as a C Corporation, but you still need to understand it.

It will affect the business environment in which you are operating.

In fact, some entities have looked into it, and have even converted to a C Corp because the 21% flat tax rate is attractive in some limited circumstances, much more so than the prior graduated tax rate that topped out at 35%.

The Tax Cuts And Jobs Act (TCJA) has reduced the Corporate Tax Rate by 40%.

We have never had a reduction in the Corporate Tax Rate of this size in the history of the Tax Code, and it is having an enormous impact on the U.S. economy.

WHAT IT IS

When we talk about the Corporate Tax Rate, the "Corporation" that we are talking about is a C Corporation, usually referred to as a C Corp.

This is a Corporation with stockholders. It accounts for its income at the corporate level, files a tax return, and pays taxes to the IRS at the corporate level.

The money left over can then be retained by the Corporation for operating capital or any other purpose. But the money can also be distributed to the stockholders, who are actually the owners of the Corporation and therefore own the retained income in the same manner that they share ownership of all other corporate assets.

If the Corporation does distribute the after-tax income, the retained income is characterized as "dividends" upon distribution, and the dividends are treated as income to the stockholders, and therefore taxable to the stockholders, although the distributed funds represent the income of the Corporation and has already been taxed once.

This is the "double taxation" characteristic of a C Corporation that people talk about, and is the primary reason for avoiding this type of entity.

But there is actually one way in which an individual might be subject to the Corporate Tax Rate even if the individual has not formed a C Corporation.

If you form a Limited Liability Company (LLC), it will be treated as a "disregarded entity" and you will report your business activity on a Schedule C or Schedule E of your Form 1040 Individual Income Tax Return.

But "disregarded entity" is actually the "default" status, which will go into effect if you do nothing on your own to file Form 8832 with the IRS and select a different method in which you would like the LLC to be taxed for the LLC activities.

You are also allowed to elect to have the LLC taxed as a Corporation, which means a C Corp, which you might not want.

The reason that people file the Election to be taxed as a Corporation is so that they can then file Form 2553 electing to be treated as a Subchapter S Corporation (Sub S or S Corp). This causes the income, deductions and credits to "pass through" the Corporation without being taxed, using Schedule K-1, and be reported on the returns of the owner or owners of the LLC.

But the Corporate Tax Rate that we are talking about is the tax rate for the standard C Corporation.

The top Corporate tax rate prior to the Tax Cuts And Jobs Act (TCJA) was 35%.

SUMMARY OF THE NEW LAW

To replace the graduated tax rate system for C Corporations which topped out at 35%, we now have a flat 21% tax rate for all C Corp income, starting with the first dollar.

NEW LAW EXPLAINED

Unlike the new tax rates for individuals, which will expire in 2025 and revert back to the prior rates if no new legislation is passed, the new Corporate Tax Rate of 21% is permanent.

This permanency was necessary in order to provide some certainty for corporations.

Corporations operate in the "long-term world," and are usually operating with a 10-year or 20-year business plan, often with losses expected in the early years, offset by large profits after that.

Facing the possibility of a reversion to a 35% top tax rate in 2025 would have killed a lot of the investment activity by C Corporations that is now happening under the TCJA.

And it is important to understand just how huge this corporate tax rate reduction really is.

You look at a reduction from 35% to 21% and you see a 14% reduction. Considering the large financial numbers we are dealing with for corporations, that is a pretty impressive amount of money that the businesses are now keeping. They are either using it to grow the business, or to pay higher dividends to the stockholders, which will then result in an increase in the Corporation's stock prices.

(Actually, it looks like the Corporations are using the extra money to buy back their own stock, and then they will use the rest to pay dividends, some of it to themselves, which will increase the price of the stock that they just bought back).

As I said, the reduction is 14%, but in reality, it is more than that.

The reduction is actually 40%.

The new rate of 21% is only 60% of the prior rate of 35%.

So, the amount of the reduction is really 40%.

I don't recall ever seeing any similar type of tax that is collected by the IRS reduced by 40%, and certainly not a type of tax that is one of the major sources of revenue.

And the "other tax" that is seldom talked about because most of the consideration about it is about how to legally manipulate it, is the Alternative Minimum Tax (AMT).

It did not apply to corporations with average annual gross receipts of less than $7.5 million for the preceding three tax years, but for the rest, it was assessed at 20%.

The AMT has now been eliminated for Corporations.

Now, let's move on to the information that will probably make you a lot of money, starting first with a new explanation of Capital Gains, and an explanation of how to calculate it under different circumstances, so that you can plan ahead for ways to pay no tax on your sales.

CHAPTER 11

CAPITAL GAINS

NEW TAX LAW

The Tax Cuts And Jobs Act (TCJA) did not change the Capital Gains Tax amounts.

The Capital Gains rates are still 0%, 15%, and 20%, but the TCJA messed with the Tax Brackets of the individual Taxpayer, as we saw in Chapter 9, so that there is actually a change in the Capital Gains structure, at least the Short Term Capital Gains.

By the way, I realize that this is not the primary reason you bought this book.

But if you are looking to be the smartest Real Estate Investor in your market, hang with me, this will help get you there.

WHAT IT IS

Capital Gains are often misunderstood.

I will provide you a clear explanation, with an Example, and you will see how to actually pay zero Capital Gains Tax, if you time it right.

Capital Gains are one of the primary concerns of Real Estate Investors, because asset appreciation is one of the two major benefits of investing in real estate. But when you sell for a profit, you also pay.

As you know, Capital Gains are taxed according to the period of time the Taxpayer owned the capital asset before selling it.

If the asset is owned for one year or less, the capital gains is characterized as Short-Term Capital Gains (STCG).

The tax rate applied to the STCG is the taxpayer's ordinary income tax bracket, from 10% to 37%.

So, STCG is always taxable.

But, Long-Term Capital Gains can actually be tax-free, because there is a 0% Tax Bracket for Long-Term Capital Gains.

And, since the TCJA reduced the tax rates and tax brackets for individuals, it could be said that the new tax law does actually lower the Capital Gains tax rate.

But that would only be true for Short-Term Capital Gains.

The tax rate for Long-Term Capital Gains (LTCG) remains the same under the new law.

LTCG are gains on assets that were sold after being owned for at least a year and one day. And those are the ones we are talking about here.

PRIOR LAW

Under the law in effect in 2017, the LTCG tax brackets were based on your ordinary income tax brackets.

It is important for you to read and understand this sub-section on Prior Law because it will help you to understand my explanation later in this Chapter about how much of your LTCG is actually taxable, and what the appropriate tax rate is.

1.) If you were previously in the 10% or the 15% ordinary income tax bracket, your LTCG was subject to 0% tax (except that some of it wasn't, see below for clarification).

2.) If you were in the 25%, 28%, 33%, or 35% ordinary income tax bracket, your LTCG was subject to 15% tax (and maybe higher on some of it).

3.) If you were in the 39.6% ordinary income tax bracket, your LTCG was subject to 20% tax.

NEW LAW EXPLAINED

Under the new tax law, there are still only three tax rates for LTCG, and they are still 0%, 15%, and 20%.

However, even though the TCJA did not change the three tax rate amounts, the TCJA did change the Capital Gains tax structure by changing the brackets for each of the tax rates by establishing cutoff points, and indexing them for inflation.

The point at which the Capital Gains tax rate changes from 0% to a 15% tax rate is:

◊ $77,200 for Married Filing Jointly (MFJ) and Surviving Spouses,

◊ $38,600 for Married Filing Separately (MFS),

◊ $51,700 for Head of Household (HH),

◊ $2,600 for estates and trusts, and

◊ $38,600 for other unmarried individuals.

The point at which the 15% tax rate changes to a 20% tax rate is:

◊ $479,000 for MFJ and Surviving Spouses,

◊ $239,500 for MFS,

◊ $452,400 for HH,

◊ $12,700 for estates and trusts, and

◊ $425,800 for other unmarried individuals.

REAL WORLD CAPITAL GAINS TAX

But the real question for Real Estate Investors, always, is how much tax you will pay.

Well, that depends on the portion of your LTCG that is taxable, combined with the rate at which it is taxable.

We have to break it down and look at a number of different calculations to answer that question.

Plow through these next few paragraphs with me, and get to the Example, which will make it all clear.

The LTCG tax rates are, in some ways, in the nature of the ordinary income tax rates, which are "marginal" tax rates, meaning that when you reach a certain level, the next dollar is taxed at a higher rate. (If you don't understand that, it doesn't matter, keep going).

If you are in the 0% LTCG tax bracket, it **does not mean that all of your LTCG is tax-free.**

To understand this, we need to look at the two categories of income that the IRS has created for organizational purposes.

They actually have more, but we only need to look at two for this calculation.

The first income category is the old basic category of ordinary taxable income.

Ordinary income is defined as income other than Capital Gains and certain Dividends.

Ordinary income is wages, salaries, tips, commissions, bonuses, and any other type of income resulting from employment, as well as interest, ordinary dividends, and net income from a sole proprietorship or from a Pass-Through Entity (PTE) such as an S Corp, LLC, or Partnership.

The second income category is Capital Gains and certain Dividends.

The ordinary income category is what the LTCG **tax brackets of 0%, 15%, and 20% are based on.**

The bracket amounts do not include your actual LTCG itself in order to determine which bracket you initially fall in.

In the world of the IRS, for purposes of taxation, the LTCG is always considered the "last" income that you received, after all of your other income, even though, in reality, you might have sold the property on January 1, and it could really be the first income you received in the tax year.

(Remember, we are playing by their rules, and we need to know what the rules are in order to use them to our advantage. Often they are not in sync with reality.)

So, let's use an Example to see how this works.

◊   You are a MFJ and your ordinary taxable income is $63,000.

◊   You sold a rent house after owning it for five years and claiming $10,000 in Depreciation.

◊   Your LTCG amount was $50,000.

So, the question is, which LTCG tax bracket are you in, and how much is your tax?

Your first inclination is to say that:

◊   your ordinary taxable income is $63,000, and

◊   that amount is less than the top (cutoff level) of the 0% tax bracket of $77,200, and

◊   therefore it does not put you into the next bracket, the 15% tax bracket,

◊   so the tax on your LTCG is 0% because you are in the 0% LTCG tax bracket.

Your second inclination is to say that:

◊   if you added your $50,000 LTCG to your $63,000 ordinary taxable income, the total would be $113,000,

◊   and put you into the 15% tax bracket,

◊   so all of your $50,000 LTCG would be taxable at 15%.

Both of those are incorrect.

It is true that you are in the 0% LTCG tax bracket because your ordinary taxable income is less than $77,200. And as long as you stay under $77,200 you will stay in the 0% bracket.

Now, here's the step in the process that is never discussed.

Your $63,000 of ordinary taxable income puts you in the 12% marginal income tax bracket for individuals.

That means that the first $19,050 of your $63,000 of ordinary taxable income will be taxed at 10%, and the remaining $43,950 will be taxed at 12%.

The total tax on your $63,000 of ordinary taxable income will be $1,905 + $5,274 = $7,179.

Now, notice that the $50,000 of LTCG will not bump you up into the 22% individual income tax bracket, because the tax brackets are only used to tax ordinary income, not Capital Gains.

But you will have to add the $50,000 to the $63,000 to find out how much of the $50,000 is taxable as LTCG.

Of course, if you read my book, "How To Do A Section 1031 Like Kind Exchange," thank you, and you will recall that the first thing that we have to do with the $50,000 of LTCG is separate out the Depreciation portion because it will be treated separately.

The entire $50,000 is classified as LTCG, but the part of it that represents the Depreciation Recapture will be taxed at a different rate from the "pure" capital gains.

You claimed $10,000 in Depreciation and now must pay a tax on that amount.

The maximum amount of tax on Depreciation Recapture is 25%.

But that still leaves $40,000 of LTCG to account for here.

How is it taxed, 0% or 15%?

Well, both.

The portion of the LTCG that will carry your ordinary taxable income amount up to the top of the 0% tax bracket of $77,200 will be taxed at 0%.

This amount is $77,200 minus $63,000 = $14,200.

There will be no tax on the first $14,200 of your $40,000 LTCG.

The remaining amount that will be taxable at 15% will be $40,000 minus $14,200 = $25,800.

This is what I meant before when I said that the LTCG tax brackets are, in some ways, "marginal" like the ordinary income tax brackets.

Of course, if you had done something like taken a year off to finish a degree, or to travel, or to serve a prison sentence (just checking to see if you're paying attention), or some similar change in your lifestyle that caused you to only have ordinary taxable income for this one year of $20,000, then your entire $50,000 of LTCG would have been non-taxable because the total of the two would be $70,000 and would still not move you out of the 0% LTCG tax bracket.

On the other hand, if your ordinary taxable income had been $83,000 instead of $63,000 all of your $50,000 LTCG would have been taxable, the Depreciation Recapture portion at 25% and the remainder at 15%, because the $83,000 moves you out of the 0% Capital Gains tax bracket.

As I have said often, knowledge of Depreciation and Capital Gains has accounted for as much as one-third of the profit that I have made from real estate investments.

Just knowing this stuff makes it possible for you to make better decisions, and to see things that other investors do not see.

I strongly encourage you to learn about these things, even if you don't find them fascinating, as I do.

After all, it is how you make money, isn't it?

Now, we will discuss what is probably the biggest gift anyone has ever given you, if you are a Real Estate Investor – the new Bonus Depreciation law.

CHAPTER 12

BONUS DEPRECIATION

NEW TAX LAW

The largest benefit in the Tax Cuts and Jobs Act might be the 20% exclusion from taxable income for Pass-Through Entities (covered in the next Chapter), but the 100% Bonus Depreciation Deduction is certainly the second largest.

The new law broadens the definition of property that qualifies for Bonus Depreciation, and also increases the maximum amounts of annual depreciation available.

It has the effect of lowering your cost of acquiring capital assets, sometimes by a lot.

It could even return the full amount of your down payment at the end of the first year of ownership.

This one law alone will make a lot of people very wealthy in the next ten years, and it will happen a lot sooner than it would have happened under the prior law.

PRIOR LAW

Except for buildings and some building improvements, Taxpayers were able to deduct 50% of the cost of new tangible personal property in the year that it was purchased and placed in service.

The remaining Basis left in the asset had to be depreciated over the assigned life of the asset, but you could start in that first year.

And the prior law only applied to new assets placed into service for the first time.

A fact that has received very little attention is that the 50% Bonus Depreciation in the prior law was about to go away. It was scheduled to be reduced to 40% in the years 2018 and 2019, and then reduced to 0% in 2020.

NEW LAW

Perhaps the greatest change in the Bonus Depreciation rule is not the increase from 50% to 100%, which is huge, but the fact that the property eligible for the new rate now includes used property.

Being able to purchase good used property instead of having to pay outrageous prices for new property, and still get Bonus Depreciation on the used property will create a lot of investments that would have otherwise been impossible.

Also, being able to deduct the entire cost of used capital assets with Bonus Depreciation instead of having to spread the cost out over the life of the asset will likely spur all types of real estate investments.

The new rule covers purchased business assets such as furniture, fixtures, appliances, equipment, computers, and similar items, with useful lives of less than 20 years.

They can usually be depreciated over 5, 7, 10, and 15 years, and the depreciation is available for the first year that the item is placed in service.

The recovery period for real estate assets like buildings exceeds 20 years, and so real estate assets do not qualify for expensing. But other associated tangible personal property may qualify.

However, like all new laws, there might be a glitch in this one.

The new law has eliminated Bonus Depreciation on a new category of property that it calls "qualified improvement property," referred to as QIP.

QIP is certain improvements to buildings that are not residential rental buildings. This category formerly included "leasehold improvements."

But this new QIP is now eligible to be treated as Section 179 property, and also has a new 15-year depreciable life instead of the 39 years that generally applies to non-residential buildings.

Of course, it is still possible that QIP will be eligible for Bonus Depreciation as well, even though it was not specifically provided for in the language of the TCJA.

Some of the other comments in the early drafting documents of the new tax law seem to indicate that it was the intention of the drafters that QIP be included in the category entitled to Bonus Depreciation, and this is shown by the fact that QIP depreciation was changed from 39 years to 15 years, thereby bringing it into the definition of "tangible personal property with a recovery period of 20 years or less," which is the definition of property eligible for Bonus Depreciation.

We still have to wait for clarification on that, and it could have a major effect on the investment value for older buildings.

The current feeling is that QIP will be qualified for Bonus Depreciation.

The Bonus Depreciation rule covers the purchase of machinery, equipment, office furniture, computer systems, software, and even vehicles.

Bonus Depreciation as it stands now will run through 2022 unless the law is extended.

Then it will begin to be phased out, dropping to 80% in 2023, 60% in 2024, 40% in 2025, 20% in 2026, and 0% after that.

Now we are ready to learn about the most confusing, and yet basically simple, part of the new TCJA, the Pass-Through Entity (PTE).

Don't worry, it's just your LLC, S Corp or Partnership.

CHAPTER 13

PASS-THROUGH ENTITIES

NEW TAX LAW

The biggest change in the new Tax Cuts And Jobs Act (TCJA) for Real Estate Investors is the way that Pass-Through Entities (PTEs) are now taxed.

Remember that the IRS defines Pass-Through Entities as "an entity that passes its income, losses, deductions, or credits to its owners, who might be partners, shareholders, beneficiaries, or investors."

Previously, the total income and credits of your LLC, Partnership, or Sub S Corp, which are the typical PTEs, were just passed through to you in their total amount, placed on your personal tax return, and taxed at your personal income level.

But it has become more complicated.

Now, we must de-construct our activities, and look at three separate questions.

1.) Is our business a Pass-Through Entity (PTE)?

2.) Is the PTE engaged in a Qualified Trade or Business (QTB)?

3.) How much of the Qualified Business Income (QBI) 20% Exclusion are we entitled to receive?

In this Chapter we will look at the PTE and answer the QTB question, and then cover QBI exclusion amount in the next Chapter.

Don't worry, you'll get used to these new terms soon. You are already familiar with the Entities involved.

Your choice of Business Entity is probably the most important decision you will ever make regarding your real estate investing career.

The choice will affect:

◊   the acquisition and disposition of real property,

◊   the construction of improvements on the property,

◊   the financing of the acquisition and improvements,

◊   the rental activities of the property,

◊   the business management of the investment, and

◊   the transfer of ownership of the property.

If you are currently an active Real Estate Investor, you need to look at the question of whether you should continue to operate in the same manner, in light of the new tax law.

If you are about to purchase your first, or next, investment property, you need to consider the choice of the best Business Entity for the endeavor.

Let's take a minute to look at the various Business Entity choices.

1.) Sole Proprietorship. You do not have any type of legal Entity structure and you are operating just as an individual. You report your income and expenses on Schedule C or Schedule E and attach it to your Form 1040 Individual Income Tax Return. You have no limit on your personal liability from things that happen in your business operations.

2.) Partnership. This is when the business operation is owned by more than one individual. Income, credits, and deductions are allocated according to percentage ownership. Liability is "joint and several" which means that each person is totally responsible for any adverse claim arising from business operations, and in some cases from the behavior of the other partner. Income and expenses are reported on Form 1065 Partnership Return of Income, and then profit/loss, credits, deduction, and other items are distributed to the partners through the use of a Schedule K-1 (Form 1065) to be reported on their individual tax returns. Partnerships may or may not have a written Partnership Agreement, and can be either a General Partnership or a Limited Partnership. An LLC with more than one member will be taxed as a General Partnership as the default classification.

3.) Limited Liability Company (LLC). This affords the individual the limit on personal liability that is available from a corporation, but without the same amount of corporate formality. The LLC can file Form 8832 and elect to be treated for tax purposes as a Partnership or as a Corporation. If choosing to be taxed as a Corporation, the LLC can file Form 2553 and elect Subchapter S status, and have the income pass through to the individual owners. The IRS actually says you can skip the filing of Form 8832 and just file Form 2553, and you will be "deemed" to have file Form 8832, but I recommend filing both forms to remove the uncertainty.

4.) Single Member Limited Liability Company (SMLLC). If the LLC has only one owner, that owner will be treated as a "disregarded entity" for tax purposes by the IRS as the default classification, and the owner can report income and expenses on Schedule C or Schedule E, the same as being a sole proprietor. But the owner can elect to be treated as a Corporation by filing the required election form. Then the owner can elect Subchapter S status and have the income pass through to be taxed at the individual level.

5.) C Corporation (C Corp). This is the most common type of business, and the one used by most public companies. The corporation issues stock which represents ownership of the company. The stockholders elect a Board of Directors to manage the company. The Board of Directors chooses company officers such as President, Vice President, Secretary, and Treasurer to run the company. The income of the company is reported at the company level and taxes are paid at the company level on the income by filing Form 1120 Corporate Tax Return. The company owns the after-tax profits. Company profits may or may not be distributed to the shareholders after each tax year, or at any time, as dividends. If dividends are paid, the shareholder then must report the dividends as income, and pay taxes, although the corporation has already been taxed on the same income, hence the term "double taxation" which is usually applied to C Corps.

6.) Professional Service Corporation (P.C.). This is a category for corporations and is reserved for use by some professionals such as doctors, architects, and attorneys. It differs from the regular corporation because it does not provide a shield against liability. It is considered to be in the public interest that these individuals be held liable for all of their conduct and activities, and should not be allowed to shield themselves from that liability through incorporation, the same way that other citizens are allowed to do, such as car salesmen, wrecker services, driveway repairmen, carpenters and plumbers, roofers, and stock brokers.

7.) S Corporation (S Corp). An S Corp is not really another type of corporation. It is actually a C Corp which has filed an election to be treated as a Subchapter S Corporation, and have the income, losses, deductions and credits flow through to the shareholders for taxation at the individual level. The S Corp actually files a corporate tax return just like a C Corp, but uses the Form 1120S, which is a Form 1120 that is adjusted for use by an S Corp. Prior to the creation of the LLC laws, the S Corp was the primary method of avoiding the double taxation of the corporate form, but still allow the individual to enjoy the limit against liability.

All of these entities except the C Corp, and the P.C. are PTEs and will be affected by the new tax law by being able to exclude up to 20% of their income from taxation.

To repeat, business income that passes through a PTE to an individual, and Sole Proprietorship income, will be taxed at the individual's tax rate, AFTER EXCLUDING UP TO 20% OF THE INCOME.

I will refer to the 20% as an "exclusion" instead of a "deduction" because it is an exclusion.

The exclusion does not apply to interest, dividend, or capital gains income, just to business income.

It sounds like a great deal, until you actually read the rule, which we will do now.

You might want to turn away at this point, this is pretty ugly.

"The deduction is the sum of the lesser of the Combined Qualified Business Income, or 20% of the excess of the taxable income divided by the sum of any net capital gain, added to the lesser of 20% of the aggregate amount of the qualified cooperative dividends of the taxpayer, or the taxable income reduced by the net capital gain."

And, the "Combined Qualified Business Income" referred to in the above explanation is defined as "the lesser of 20% of the qualified business income with respect to the qualified trade or business, or the greater of 50% of the W-2 wages with respect to the qualified trade or business, or the sum of 25% of the W-2 wages with respect to the qualified trade or business, plus 2.5% of the unadjusted basis immediately after acquisition of all qualified property."

Did you get that?

Have you ever read such gibberish?

This new rule is a pig's breakfast, because the IRS always writes everything starting with the backend, or the exceptions.

But this can actually be explained, IN PLAIN ENGLISH, and I will do so in the next Chapter.

The first thing that we need to understand here is that there has been a change in terminology that has confused the explanation.

The rule talks about "Qualified Business Income" and you would naturally think that the term means "business income" that somehow needs to be "qualified," as in "qualified business income."

It does not mean that.

The PTEs that I told you about above that now qualify for the exclusion of 20% of their income from taxation, are now being referred to as a "Qualified Business" instead of being a PTE that is engaged in a "Qualified Trade or Business (QTB)."

In other words, they are "businesses" that "qualify" for the 20% income exclusion; hence "Qualified Business Income," meaning that the income is from a qualified business.

So, "Qualified Business Income" just means the income from a Pass-Through Entity (PTE), now called a "Qualified Business."

So, just think "PTE" and "20% income exclusion."

Let's move on to the next Chapter and find out how to calculate this income amount and the exclusion amount.

I'll have some great Examples that will make it clear.

CHAPTER 14

QUALIFIED BUSINESS INCOME

NEW TAX LAW

"Qualified Business Income" (QBI) is the income from a "qualified trade or business."

A "qualified trade or business," as explained in the prior Chapter, is a Pass-Through Entity (PTE).

A Pass-Through Entity (PTE) is "an entity that passes its income, losses, deductions, or credits to its owners, who might be partners, shareholders, beneficiaries, or investors."

There are certain "service trades or businesses" which do not qualify as a "qualified trade or business," and we won't go into them here, because the renting of real property and real estate development both meet the definition of "qualified trade or business."

And QBI does not include interest, dividends, or capital gains.

QBI only includes the income from the operation of the qualified business.

The new Tax Cuts And Jobs Act (TCJA) provides for and exemption from taxation for up to 20% of the income of the QBI.

If your total taxable income from all sources is $50,000, and your QBI portion of that is $40,000, you can exclude $8,000 from taxation, which is 20% of the $40,000 QBI.

Nice and simple so far.

But this is where it starts getting more complicated (and it never stops).

You might not be able to take the entire 20%, because there are limitations and exclusions.

The limitations and exclusions start with the Threshold Amount.

The Threshold Amount is the income amount that you must be under in order to qualify for the flat 20%.

The Threshold Amount is $157,500 for individual taxpayers, and it is $315,000 for married taxpayers filing jointly (MFJ).

These amounts are not your QBI amount, this is your total taxable income.

If your total taxable income is below the Threshold Amount, your QBI exclusion amount is simply 20% of the QBI for each of your qualified businesses, determined on a "per business," not a "per taxpayer," basis.

But the Exclusion takes place at the individual taxpayer level. The PTE itself cannot qualify for the Exclusion amount, so the PTE just passes the entire amount of income through to the taxpayer.

And if you are below the Threshold Amount, you don't have to deal with the complications contained in the remainder of the rule. You're finished.

But if your taxable income is above the Threshold Amount, you are still eligible for the Exclusion, but there is a second "exclusion" that you must also calculate.

You are only entitled to take the smaller of the two exclusions, the 20% exclusion, or the new exclusion amount.

Your new exclusion is called the "wage and capital limit."

The "wage and capital limit" is the greater of either:

1.) 50% of W-2 wages with respect to your trade or business, or

2.) the sum of 25% of these W-2 wages, plus 2.5% of the unadjusted basis, immediately after acquisition, of all qualified property.

"Qualified property" is tangible property subject to depreciation and available for use in your business at the end of the tax year, and used in the production of the QBI.

I know that sounds like gibberish, but here's what it means in Plain English.

Let's do an Example.

You are Married, Filing Jointly (MFJ) and your total taxable income is $350,000.

Your QBI is $75,000.

Your W-2 wages are $20,000.

Your qualified property is $160,000.

Your 20% exclusion of the $75,000 QBI would be $15,000 if you were not over the Threshold Amount. But you are. Your $350,000 taxable income puts you $35,000 over the $315,000 Threshold Amount for MFJ.

So, at this point, you must calculate the two factors in your new second exclusion amount.

For the first one, 50% of your W-2 wages of $20,000 is $10,000.

For the second one, 25% of your W-2 wages ($5,000) added to 2.5% of your qualified property of $160,000 ($4,000) is $9,000.

Your new exclusion amount is $10,000 because that is the greater of the two amounts that you just calculated.

And since the new exclusion amount of $10,000 is lower than the 20% exclusion amount of $15,000, you must now claim the new lower exclusion amount of $10,000.

But you don't get the entire amount like you would if your total taxable income was just $1 over the Threshold Amount, instead of $35,000 over.

There is a Phase Out Period that runs up to $100,000 over the Threshold Amount. During this period, the exclusion amount is prorated.

The Phase Out Period for MFJ taxpayers starts at $315,000 and goes up to $415,000, at which point the exclusion disappears altogether.

To find out where you are, we take your total taxable income of $350,000 and subtract $315,000, the Threshold Amount, and get $35,000. This is where you are on that $100,000 Phase Out line, the $35,000 point.

Then we divide $35,000 by the $100,000 and we get 35%.

Then we multiply 35% times the $10,000 exclusion that we calculated, and we get the amount of the exclusion that we are not entitled to because of the level of total taxable income being $350,000.

That means that we are still entitled to 65% of the $10,000.

And 65% of the $10,000 exclusion is $6,500.

This is the amount of our exclusion at this total income level and with this set of factors.

I hope this helps you understand this mess.

Now remember that we still have the "technical corrections" that will be coming out during the next two years to explain or expand on the rule, and eventually we will have the Treasury Regulations that will also explain the rule, using Examples.

CHAPTER 15

ENTITY CONVERSION

OVERVIEW

Maybe you have already formed a Business Entity and you want to change it, either because:

◊ you realize that you should have started with a different one, or

◊ the new Tax Cuts And Jobs Act (TCJA) has provided some business advantages or tax advantages for another Entity, that your Entity does not have.

You can change the Entity.

It might not be practical to do so, but you <u>can</u> do it.

The word normally used is "convert," as in, "You can convert the business entity to another one."

But this does not mean what it sounds like it means.

The act of "conversion" is just one of your options.

There are four actions you can take if you no longer want to operate the entity that you are operating, but want to continue to own and operate your business, just using a different Entity.

You can:

1.) Continue the day-to-day operation of the business, but change over the form of the Business Entity, say from an LLC to a S Corp. This is called a "conversion," and sometimes a "statutory conversion" because it is done under State statute (law).

2.) Form the new Business Entity that you want to use, and then combine it with your existing Business Entity. This is a "merger."

3.) Stop operating your existing business, distribute the assets to the owners or shareholders, and then use the assets, and perhaps new money, to form the Business Entity that you want. This is called "dissolution and formation."

4.) Form a new Business Entity which will purchase the assets of your existing Business Entity, including the name, goodwill, and contracts, and continue the business activity. This is called an "asset sale."

I will cover each one below.

But keep in mind that when you do anything with an existing entity, you have four considerations:

1.) Approval of all of the owners of interest, no matter how small.

2.) Assignment of contracts and agreements involving outside parties.

3.) Following all of the IRS rules for the procedure, and then reporting everything.

4.) Following all State laws.

Now let's look at your options.

CONVERSION

Most states have laws in place that provide for changing one type of Entity into another type of Entity.

The problem with these laws is that the requirements have become so bloated in order to cover every conceivable type of situation, that they are usually not workable for regular situations.

You must start with explaining the intended transaction in a Plan of Conversion, and then, depending on your situation, you proceed with a:

1.) Resolution of Shareholders Authorizing the Plan.

2.) Resolution of Board of Directors Authorizing the Plan.

3.) Minutes of Meeting of Shareholders Approving the Plan.

4.) Minutes of Meeting of Board of Directors Approving the Plan.

5.) Certificate of Conversion.

6.) Certificate of Formation.

7.) Etc.

After all that, some of the paperwork must be filed with the State to be approved.

Then you can start all over again explaining it all to the IRS and reporting any income, or transfer of assets, and depreciation (and depreciation recapture).

Please understand that you are doing a Conversion under State law, and that law is not intended to help you do what you are trying to do. That State law is written to protect all of the affected parties from <u>what you might do that is detrimental to their interests.</u>

Compare all of this to being able to create a new LLC in about 30 minutes, and you see why Conversion will probably be done only as a last resort.

A Warning Here: be careful in getting your information from the internet. Most of those websites are owned by companies who are trying to charge you money to do a Statutory Conversion for you, and they want you to think that it is a great idea and very easy to do. This is not usually the case. If you decide to do a Conversion, hire an actual Business Attorney licensed to practice law in the State involved.

MERGER

A Merger occurs when you form a new business entity, and then merge the existing entity into it. It depends on State law, but what probably happens in a Merger is that all of the assets of the existing business entity are transferred into the new business entity, and the existing business entity ceases to exist.

State law will probably dictate that:

◊ The existing entity will cease to exist as a legal entity.

◊ The assets of the existing entity will be vested in the new entity.

◊ The liabilities of the existing entity will be assumed by the new entity.

◊ The owners of the existing entity will become the owners of the new entity.

The exact details of your Merger will depend on the laws of the State in which you are operating.

Whether or not you want to do a Merger will depend on what you are trying to accomplish.

One of the things to consider is that after the Merger, the owners of the new entity are still liable for any claims that might me made against the original entity. This would not be the case with a Dissolution and Formation, or with an Asset Sale.

Also, the IRS wants to be involved in a Merger, and has special rules for reporting everything that has taken place, and accounting for any change in income allocation, debt relief, depreciation recapture, etc.

Sometimes a Merger is the only option open for the specific situation, and often that is the only reason for doing one.

But it can be very expensive and very time-consuming.

DISSOLUTION AND FORMATION

Companies can cease operation at any time, and many of them do every year.

Most are on the calendar year accounting period and on the calendar year tax year, and so the end date is usually December 31.

Many of the companies are small businesses with a single owner, and maybe a spouse, and they simply cease operations.

Other companies involve more than one owner, such as a Corporation with Shareholders, an LLC with Members, or a Partnership with Partners.

In these latter cases it is necessary to look at the documents of formation for the entity to determine the process involved is dissolution, and to follow those steps.

In most cases, it will be required that for a Corporation, the Board of Directors will adopt a Resolution To Dissolve, and then the Shareholders will vote to approve it. The documents will be entered into the Minute Book, and then the required documentation will be sent to the State notifying them of the dissolution.

For an LLC, the same formalities are usually not required, but there must be documentation of the decision and of the approval of members.

The process should be outlined in the Operating Agreement.

The important thing to note here is that this is a simple procedure, without all of the State-mandated "jumping through hoops" involved in a "Statutory Conversion" and a "Merger," and yet those two procedures dominate the information available on the web.

As I said before, that is because the web content is being provided by companies that want to sell you a product or service, and that is great. It is the new world of business, and it supports the environment that we all enjoy on the internet.

Just think about Dissolution as a reasonable alternative to the complex process involved in a Conversion or Merger, and make a rational decision.

And, of course, once you have dissolved the existing entity, you are free to form the new entity that meets all of your new requirements.

You can see the Chapters above for the process involved in that.

There is one more possible route, the Asset Sale, and it is my personal favorite.

ASSET SALE

If you are ever in a situation of considering an offer to buy your company, and the Buyer has an Attorney who understands business law, you will be told that instead of actually buying your company, the Buyer wants to buy the assets of your company.

The reason that the Buyer is being advised to do this instead of just buying all of your stock and continuing to operate the business, is a matter of liability.

The Buyer does not want to assume any liability for things that might have happened in the past that he knows nothing about, but that the company is still liable for.

If he simply buys all of the company assets and uses them in his own company, even if he uses the same name (providing certain public and private notices are done), same address, etc., it is the same as starting a new company.

But he has a profitable company already up and running, with customers, with brand recognition and Goodwill.

And you can do the same thing. You can actually form a new business Entity that buys your existing business Entity.

You can form an LLC and have it buy the assets of your C Corporation or S Corp or Partnership.

Or you can form a C Corporation, elect Sub S status, and have it buy the assets of your LLC.

You do not need the State's approval for this, and you really do not need the approval of the IRS.

However, you will need to document the asset sale for purposes of reporting it to the IRS, but the process is not much more than what you would be doing in the ordinary course of business.

And you will need an Accountant who knows all of the odd laws regarding asset sale and what it might trigger.

After your existing Entity sells all of the assets and files the tax return, you can distribute the net sales proceeds to the owners just as you would distribute any income.

What you do next will depend on the advice you get from your Attorney, but what is often done is to continue to have the inactive entity exist for a few years, filing "zero" tax returns each year, and then mark the last return as "Final Return" and do nothing after that.

The intervening time period will exhaust the Statute of Limitations on most possible claims against the Entity, which would not be a problem anyway since it has no assets, but would prevent the claims from being filed against the owners, which would be the case if the Entity had been dissolved.

CONCLUSION

You might no longer want to operate the business entity that you are operating, but want to continue with your business, just using a different type of entity.

There are four ways that you can do this.

1.) Conversion.

2.) Merger.

3.) Dissolution and Formation.

4.) Asset Sale.

The bulk of the information available to you on the web might lead you to think that the first two, Conversion and Merger, are the most common and preferred methods.

This is not the case.

They are more complicated and more expensive, and require more time and involvement of third parties and authorities.

The use of the last two, with the help of a good Attorney, will often provide the better route for you to accomplish your goal in the manner best for you.

No two situations are the same, but the new provisions in the Tax Cuts And Jobs Act affect every single business in the country.

And there might be some significant advantages for you operating under a different business entity.

CHAPTER 16

REAL ESTATE PROFESSIONAL

OVERVIEW

Being a Real Estate Professional has nothing to do with how well you know real estate, or whether your investments are making money and increasing in value.

It doesn't mean "professional" in the sense of how well you do what you do.

The IRS uses this definition to describe the amount of time you are spending on real estate, and the type of activity in which you are engaged.

The IRS then uses the determination of Real Estate Professional to dictate which type of losses you will be allowed to deduct, and which type of other income you will be allowed to offset with those losses.

In most cases, you will probably want to prove that you meet the qualifications for being considered a Real Estate Professional, because there are many advantages. I will explain those later.

It's very odd. The Internal Revenue Code does not actually refer to individuals as Real Estate Professionals if they meet the test.

But the term is used by the U.S. Tax Court, by IRS Publications, and is contained in the Treasury Regulations.

So, it is real. And you do need to deal with it.

Let me give you the definition first and then I will tell you when and where it becomes critical.

DEFINITION

The definition of Real Estate Professional is <u>broken into two parts</u>.

<u>You must meet both definitions</u> to be placed in this category.

FIRST PART

You must perform more than 750 hours of personal services during the tax year (which is usually the calendar year) in real property trades (plural) or businesses (plural) in which you materially participate. (I will explain "materially participate" later.)

To put this into usable perspective, 750 hours annually is:

◊   62.5 hours monthly,

◊   14.42 hours weekly, and

◊   2.89 hours each day (a 5-day work week).

And you might be able to include all of your real estate activities in meeting the 750-hour requirement, not just your real estate rental activities.

Section 469(c)(7)(C) says that the term "real estate trade or business" includes:

◊ Any real property development.
◊ Any real property redevelopment.
◊ Construction.
◊ Reconstruction.
◊ Acquisition.
◊ Conversion.
◊ Rental.
◊ Operation.
◊ Management.
◊ Leasing.
◊ Brokerage.

So you can count all of these activities.

Next, you have to meet the test for "material participation," which requires satisfying at least one of the 7 tests contained in Temp. Regs. Sec. 1.469T(a).

You will find the entire text of the law at:

Www.law.cornell.edu/cfr/text/26/1.469-5T.

I recommend that you read it. It is highly informative. The text is cumbersome, being written in "IRS double negative," but the Examples are some of the best I have ever seen, and that is why I put the link here. You might even find an Example that describes your situation.

And one thing that you absolutely must do is keep good records.

The IRS loves to use the word "contemporaneous," meaning at the time that you did it.

I once told a Tax Examiner, "If I am the type of person who will falsify a record, I am just as likely to do it contemporaneously as I am three months later."

And I believe that to be true of most people.

He said, "We find that not to be the case."

So, you'll be helping yourself a great deal if you keep a log recording all of your activities, and keep copies of anything else that will prove them.

Understand, IRS agents love to close cases. It makes them look good. And they will do it if you give them something to put in the file.

That's very important, because someone else will be reviewing their work, and the fact that the Agent believes you is just not going to be enough. They need something to show their Supervisor.

So, there you have it.

And if you cannot satisfy the 750-hour requirement, or you cannot prove "material participation," you cannot qualify as a Real Estate Professional, regardless of everything else. You're done.

If you meet the first part of the test, we move on.

SECOND PART

More than 50% of the total personal services that you perform in trades or businesses must be in real property trades of businesses in which you materially participate.

Before we look at how to meet the 50% threshold, let's look at the definition of "materially participate" to see if <u>what</u> you are doing even qualifies.

The most important element of "materially participate" is the fact that the determination is made <u>for each separate property</u> that you own, unless you elect to treat all of your separate rental real estate interests as a single rental real estate activity.

This is probably something that you should do.

Otherwise, you might be a Real Estate Professional regarding the Duplex, the beach condo, and the retail store, but not a Real Estate Professional for the apartment building, the rent houses, or the townhouses.

Combine them all together.

The election to do so is made under Section 469(c)(7). The process is to simply file a statement making the election with your income tax return.

The election can even be made late by filing an amended return.

Now, how do we meet the 50% threshold?

First, understand that if you have a full-time job working 40 hours a week in a non-real estate activity, it is unlikely that you will be able to show that you also worked more than 40 hours in your own real estate activities, and materially participated.

However, if you are a freelancer or independent contractor, or if you are a solopreneur who only works when someone hires you and these activities are real estate activities, you might be able to qualify.

If you are married and file a joint tax return, either you or your spouse must qualify as a Real Estate Professional by meeting both requirements.

Now that you have qualified, let's look at why it matters.

WHY IT MATTERS

One of the major advantages of owning investment real estate is that you can have "paper" losses without actually losing any money, and you want to be able to deduct these losses from the rest of your income, and eliminate the taxes on that other income.

But losses from real estate rental activity are passive losses under the Internal Revenue Code, and can be used to offset passive income, but cannot be used to offset income that you receive from "non-passive" activities.

This rule applies to all of your rental real estate activities even if you are actually heavily involved. The losses are considered "per se" passive losses.

If your Modified Adjusted Gross Income (MAGI) is less than $100,000 you can claim up to $25,000 of passive rental losses against other passive income.

If your MAGI is above $100,000 the $25,000 amount is reduced by $1 for each $2 of income. MAGI of $110,000 is $10,000 above $100,000 and would reduce your $25,000 allowable by $5,000 and you could only offset $20,000 of other passive income.

At $150,000 MAGI, you are unable to claim any of your passive losses.

The unclaimed losses must be carried over to future years.

If you sell the rental property and still have unused passive losses, you can deduct them from the profit on the sale.

However, if you qualify as a Real Estate Professional, your rental real estate activity is not automatically considered a passive activity.

And if you materially participate in the activity, then you can deduct any losses against your other non-passive income, such as W-2 wages.

And, of course, if the losses are considered non-passive losses, the income is considered non-passive income, and can also be offset by other non-passive losses.

A Real Estate Professional's income from real estate rentals is also excluded from the definition of self-employment income, and is not subject to the 15.3% additional SE Tax.

It is also removed from the "net investment income" category and is not subject to that 3.8% tax assessed on taxpayers with a Modified Adjusted Gross Income above a certain level.

CONCLUSION

Qualifying as a Real Estate Professional is a very big deal.

Depending on your particular situation, it can have a huge impact on your tax liability.

If you do plan to qualify, you should be very prudent in documenting your activities in detail as you perform them, or very soon thereafter.

"Contemporaneous" does not mean immediately. It means "at about the same time."

You should also make the election to group all of your rental real estate activities together.

To strengthen your case, you should also keep phone records, credit card receipts, and invoices. Those are hard to dispute.

And, of course, one thing that is often overlooked if that if you don't want to claim the status, even though you qualify, you don't have to.

It just gives you the added advantage of deciding which way you want to go.

CHAPTER 17

FLIPPING PROPERTIES

OVERVIEW

One area of Real Estate Investing that sets itself apart from the others is the practice of buying real estate, rehabilitating it, and then selling it for profit.

It has come to be known as "Flipping Properties."

It is a short-term activity, and distinctly different from the form of investing known as "Buy and Hold," which involves buying real estate, possibly rehabilitating it, and then renting or leasing it to tenants over a number of years in return for rental income, with the added bonus of property value appreciation.

Investing in rental real estate is considered a passive activity, with passive income and losses, unless you are a Real Estate Professional. See Chapter 16.

But, if you are flipping properties you will probably be considered by the IRS to be a real estate "dealer."

Even if some of the properties are held in your name for more than 12 months before they are sold, you still cannot claim Long Term Capital Gains status on the income.

The properties will still be considered "inventory for sale" if the dominant characteristic of your business activities is "buying and selling real estate."

You are a dealer.

You are operating a business, just like a furniture store.

Your income will be taxable as ordinary business income.

And this could significantly increase your tax liability.

You have been ensnared by the Self-Employment Tax rule.

SELF-EMPLOYMENT TAX

If you operate your flipping business in your own name, the net income will be reported to the IRS on Schedule C of your personal income tax return, your Form 1040, and will be taxed according to your individual income tax bracket.

In addition to the income tax, you will also pay a Self-Employment (SE) Tax.

The SE Tax replaces the Social Security Tax and Medicare Tax amounts that would be deducted from your W-2 wages if you were a Statutory Employee.

The SE Tax total is 15.3%.

It is made up of 12.4% Social Security Tax and 2.9% Medicare Tax.

However, you can save a great deal of taxes by operating your business as one of the legal entities available to you, such as an LLC, S Corp or Partnership.

We will look at that next.

CHOICE OF ENTITY

You can review all of the options above, but I will tell you that the best of the options for flipping properties is to operate your business as a Subchapter S Corporation, also called a Sub S, or as we will call it, an S Corp.

You can become an S Corp in one of two ways.

The first way is to form a standard corporation, called a C Corporation, or C Corp.

After creating the C Corp, you can file Form 2553 with the IRS, electing to be treated for tax purposes as an S Corp.

The second way of becoming an S Corp is to create a Limited Liability Company (LLC).

Then, instead of accepting the default status of being treated for tax purposes as a Disregarded Entity, you file Form 8832 Entity Classification Election, electing to be treated for tax purposes as a Corporation.

But be careful!

You are now a C Corp, and you don't want to be.

You must now file Form 2553 Election By Small Business Corporation, mentioned above, to have the LLC treated for tax purposes as an S Corp.

Please note that the Instructions for Form 8832, Entity Classification Election, says:

"An eligible entity that timely files Form 2553 to elect classification as an S corporation and meets all other requirements to qualify as an S corporation is deemed to have made an election under Regulations section 301.7701-3(c)(v) to be classified as an association taxable as a corporation."

I am not comfortable with that. If the Form 2553 is not "timely" filed, or if the IRS claims that it wasn't, then your LLC is not "deemed to have made an election" ... "to be classified as an association taxable as a corporation," and therefore your S Corp status is questionable.

What I do is just file Form 8832, then Form 2553, and there are never any questions.

But it is a decision that you should make for yourself.

Now that your business is an S Corp, you can treat your income differently for tax purposes.

S CORP

The S Corp will pay you a W-2 salary and will withhold your portion of the Social Security and Medicare taxes (we are ignoring other small miscellaneous withholding, like Unemployment Taxes).

If you are the only Shareholder/Owner, the S Corp will distribute the remainder of the annual income to you.

The income that "drops through" from the S Corp to the Shareholder/Owner **is not considered Self-Employment Income, so there is no 15.3% tax to be paid to the IRS.**

This is your tax savings with the S Corp!

Let's look at an Example to see the actual tax savings numbers.

(Note: there is a Medicare Surtax of 0.9% levied on Taxpayers with incomes above a computed "Threshold Amount," some as low as $125,000, but we don't have enough information about our individual Taxpayer to include this computation.)

Now, for our Example.

First, I will do the numbers for a Sole Proprietor, and then an S Corp.

Your total income is $130,000.00.

If you are a Sole Proprietor or if you have formed an LLC and chosen to be treated for tax purposes as a Disregarded Entity, you will pay the highest tax.

First, you are allowed a 20% QBI Deduction of $26,000 under the new IRC Section 199A in the Tax Cuts And Jobs Act.

This reduces your Taxable Income to $104,000.

You are single and you take the Standard Itemized Deduction of $12,000.

This reduces your Taxable Income to $92,000.

We are ready to add up your taxes.

Your tax of 10% on the first $9,525 is $952.50.

Your tax of 12% on the next $29,175 is $3,501.

Your tax of 22% on the next $43,800 is $9,636.

Your tax of 24% on the next $9,500 is $2,280.

Your total income tax liability on the Taxable Income of $92,000 is 952.50 + 3,501 + 9,636 + 2,280 = $16,369.50.

This is an Effective Tax Rate of 17.8%.

But there is more.

Since you are a Sole Proprietor and therefore self-employed, you will be subject to the Self-Employment (SE) Tax.

The new Section 199A created by the Tax Cuts And Jobs Act is part of Chapter One of the Internal Revenue Code, which covers income taxation.

But the SE Tax is contained in Chapter Two of the Code, and therefore the Section 199A Qualified Business Income 20% Exemption does not apply to your Adjusted Gross Income or Self-Employment Income on which the SE Tax is based, so we are dealing with the entire $130,000.00.

The SE Tax is actually a combination of two taxes, which total 15.3%.

The taxes are the Social Security Tax and the Medicare Tax.

The Social Security Tax is 12.4% of the SE Income of the Taxpayer up to a maximum of $128,400.

The Medicare Tax is 2.9% of all Earned Income and there is no limit.

So, $128,400 of your $130,000 SE Income is taxed as 12.4%, for a total of $15,921.60.

And all of your $130,000 SE Income is taxed at 2.9%, for a total of $3,770.

Your total SE Tax is $19,691.60.

You will notice that this is actually more than your total income tax, even though you are in the 24% marginal tax bracket.

Your total tax on the $130,000 is $36,061.10, which is an Effective Tax Rate of 27.7%.

Now let's look at what your taxes would be under the same scenario if you were operating as an S Corp.

The S Corp is required to pay you reasonable compensation as an employee for the work that you do even if you are the owner, or one of the owners.

The first determination is what amount of "reasonable compensation" should the S Corp pay you. The IRS provides no guidance except that it should be "reasonable."

Many Taxpayers think that this means it should be a reasonable percentage of the total income or net income of the business, and that is not correct. It is more than that.

"Reasonable compensation" means that all of the circumstances of the business enterprise should be taken into consideration.

If a Salesman has a company that sells the products of other companies, the income will depend almost entirely on his ability and efforts.

"Reasonable compensation" for him would be very high.

But if the company income is generated mostly by the physical assets of the company, and as a return on the financial investment and associated risk, and the owner just manages the operation, then "reasonable compensation" for him will be a much lower amount.

So, let's settle on a salary of $40,000 for you from the S Corp.

As the S Corp pays your salary, it will deduct the $40,000 as a business expense, and reduce the $130,000 total income in our Example to $90,000.

But the S Corp will have additional expenses to deduct, brought about by the payment of the salary.

In addition to paying your salary, the S Corp will deduct and withhold from your salary the estimated amount of your income tax liability. This income tax withholding amount will be sent to the IRS.

But the S Corp will also send to the IRS the amount of Social Security Tax and Medicare Tax required for your salary amount.

Social Security Tax is 12.4% and Medicare Tax is 2.9%.

But only half of these amounts will be taken out of your salary. The S Corp will have to pay the other half.

You will have 6.2% deducted from your salary for the Social Security Tax. That is $2,480.00.

You will have 1.45% deducted from your salary for Medicare Tax. That is $580.00.

The total is $3,060.00.

The S Corp will have to pay a matching amount of $3,060.00.

This will reduce the S Corp total income to $86,940.00.

Now let's calculate the Net Income of the S Corp, which will "pass through" to you as the sole Shareholder/ Owner.

First, the S Corp is entitled to the 20% Qualified Business Income Exemption under Section 199A of the Internal Revenue Code, created by the Tax Cuts And Jobs Act (TCJA).

The Exemption amount is actually "up to 20% of the Qualified Business Income," and only individual Taxpayers with AGI under $157,000.00 are entitled to the full 20%. If you are over that amount, there is another calculation for you.

Section 199A is a complicated new law, and I explain it in two Chapters in my book "Tax Cuts And Jobs Act For Real Estate Investors: The New Rules," available at www.amazaon.com/Michael-Lantrip/e/B01N2ZRGUY.

The 20% Exemption that the S Corp is entitled to here is $17,388.00.

That leaves the corporate Net Taxable Income at $69,552.00.

This is the amount that passes through to you on the Schedule K-1 from the Form 1120S, U.S. Income Tax Return for an S Corporation.

Now we are ready to calculate your personal tax liability.

You have two income sources.

The first is your salary as reported on your W-2, and that amount is $40,000.00.

The second is your K-1 income, which is $69,552.00.

You have already paid your Social Security Taxes and your Medicare Taxes on your salary.

Your K-1 income is not considered self-employment income, so there is no SE Tax due, although there is some authority for assessing the 2.9% Medicare Tax, which we will not do.

So, let's calculate your tax liability.

Your total income is $109,552.00.

Your tax of 10% on the first $9,525.00 is $952.00.

Your tax of 12% on the next $29,175.00 is $3,501.00.

Your tax of 22% on the next $43,800.00 is $9,636.00.

Your tax of 24% on the next $27,052.00 is $6,492.48.

Your total income tax liability is 952.50 + 3,501.00 + 9,636.00 + 6,492.48 = $20,581.98.

Add to this the $2,480.00 Social Security Tax and the $580.00 Medicare Tax that was deducted from your wages, and your total out-of-pocket is $23,641.98.

Looking back to the calculations for operating as a Sole Proprietor, you will see that your total out-of-pocket was $36,061.10 on the same $130,000 income.

So, no only does the S Corp provide you with a shield against personal liability, but it also saves you $12,419.12 in taxes.

CONCLUSION

If you are flipping properties, you are different from all other Real Estate Investors.

You are more like someone running a retail store.

You are operating a business.

You are able to use any of the legal entities in the book to operate your activities, but it just makes sense to use the S Corp.

And another matter that we have not considered, but should do so now, is whether you should use a new Entity for each property that you flip.

You can legally use the same Entity over and over again.

But here's what could happen.

You have just completed a huge project, made $200,000, have a contract and are ready to close.

You are sued for an asbestos-cancer claim over a little $15,000 deal that you did years ago when you were first starting out, using the same Entity that you are now using.

If you lose the lawsuit, you will lose everything that you have inside the Entity, which includes the current project, even though the lawsuit is about a property you sold five years ago.

And if you guaranteed any of the borrowed funds on the current project, you are on the hook for those as well.

You might consider using a new Entity each time that you purchase a new project.

When you sell a property, just go dormant with the Entity, and wait for four to six years, depending on when the Statute of Limitations on the most likely claims are in your State, and then use the Entity again.

And do not just dissolve the Entity after the property is sold, because that will just transfer the liability from the Entity to you personally.

Of course, this involves more expense that you would want, but it provides protection against liability.

Legal and accounting costs are just two of the expenses of doing business, and they are often the ones that provide you the most benefit.

What do you think is a reasonable amount to pay for protecting all of your business assets plus the rehab costs and potential profit in your current project?

With lawsuits, it is not a matter of if, but a matter of when.

CHAPTER 18

CHARGING ORDERS

WHAT IT IS

A Charging Order (CO) is an Order issued by a Court and signed by a Judge, directed to an individual or legal entity that is holding funds, or controls the distribution of funds, for a second individual.

The Charging Order directs the first individual or entity to transfer the funds to a third party instead of transferring them to the second individual who owns them.

This comes about when there has been a lawsuit filed against the owner of the funds, and the lawsuit has resulted in a Judgment being granted against the owner of the funds.

The holder of the Judgment lien is called the Judgment Creditor, and the party against whom the Judgment is entered is called the Judgment Debtor.

The Judgment filing creates a Lien on all of the non-exempt assets of the Judgment Debtor.

But if the asset involved is an ownership interest in a Limited Liability Company (LLC) or a Limited Partnership (LP), then the asset cannot be taken (in most States).

That's where the Charging Order comes in.

The unique feature of the Charging Order is that it does not grant the Judgment Creditor the right to receive the asset, but only the right to receive payments or distributions that the Judgment Debtor would receive representing the income produced by the asset.

So, the Charging Order is a court-ordered lien on the distributions, not on the asset.

Charging Order protection is not available for the entity itself if the entity is sued and has a Judgment granted against it.

HOW IT WORKS

For Example, you and your brother are contractors, and together you set up an LLC to run your business.

But your brother gets into financial trouble with a personal debt, is sued, and has a Judgment entered against him for $100,000.

It is not a Judgment against the LLC, but your brother owns half of the interest in the LLC as one of his assets. And his assets are subject to being taken to satisfy the Judgment.

However, under the Charging Order protection, the interest in the LLC cannot be taken, only the distribution represented by the interest.

So, if the LLC makes $120,000 in the tax year, you and your brother will each receive a Schedule K-1 (1065) for $60,000 of income.

(You did not file Form 8832 electing the way in which you wanted to be treated for tax purposes, so you were give the default category of Partnership by the IRS).

But since your brother is not entitled to receive his $60,000 of income because of the Charging Order, his Schedule K-1 is sent to the holder of the Judgment Lien under the terms of the Charging Order.

WHY IT IS VALUABLE

However, the Charging Order does not actually require that the distribution of the income be made to the holder of the Judgment Lien, the Judgment Creditor.

The Charging Order requires that <u>when and if</u> the distribution is made, it must be made to the Judgment Creditor instead of your brother, the Judgment Debtor.

And the Charging Order does not give the Judgment Creditor any voting rights or any other rights regarding the LLC.

Also, a copy of the Schedule K-1 will be sent to the IRS identifying the Judgment Creditor as the Taxpayer entitled to receive the $60,000 of income.

The IRS will expect the Judgment Creditor to report the income on his personal tax return and pay the taxes on the $60,000 of income, even if he did not actually receive the income.

If the Member Managers of the LLC, which are you and your brother, decide not to distribute your brother's portion of the income, the Judgment Creditor will end up paying thousands of dollars in taxes on income that he may never receive.

Then you can go through it again next year.

Eventually, he will release the lien on the LLC interest, or, more likely, his Attorney will not file for the Charging Order in the first place.

This is why Charging Order protection is valuable.

HOW IT COULD FAIL

The laws concerning the Limited Liability Company (LLC), the Limited Partnership (LP), and the laws concerning Charging Orders are different for each State.

In some states, the Charging Order is seen as a protection device for those owners of an interest in an LLC and LP who have not had a Judgment Lien filed against them, but one of the other interest owners in the LLC or LP has had a Judgment Lien filed.

In other states, the Charging Order is seen as a reasonable and responsible business rule, and should be afforded to all owners of LLCs and LPs.

Wyoming and Nevada are probably the best, but first let's discuss the worst.

There are some states that even deny Charging Order protection to Single Member LLCs (SMLLCs). I discuss those below.

There are 15 States which will allow the holder of the Judgment Lien to petition the Court for permission to foreclose on the LLC and LP interest, if the Court can be convinced that the Charging Order is not a reasonable solution.

In addition to allowing judicial foreclosure of the LLC and LP interest, some States also provide for the appointment of a Receiver. This is a disaster for both parties, as the Receiver may just try to keep the matter going for as long as possible and collect the fees.

But you can protect yourself against these situations.

If you operate in one of the States with weak Charging Order protection, you can create the LLC in that State and have it own the real estate.

But you can have the LLC owned by another LLC that you create in a State with strong Charging Order protections, like Texas, Wyoming, Michigan, or Nevada.

This way, you don't own the LLC that owns the real estate.

You own the LLC that owns the LLC that owns the real estate.

Then, when there is a Judgment Lien against you, the LLC interest that you own is an LLC formed in a State with strong Charging Order protection, and your interest in that LLC cannot be taken.

You can only be subjected to a Charging Order, and you can just leave the income in the LLC that your LLC owns. Even though it is in a State with weak Charging Order protection, it is safe because it is owned by your LLC, not by you, and so it is not affected by either the Judgment or the Charging Order.

The Charging Order can only be against the interest that the Judgment Debtor owns in the LLC created in the State with strong protection, and that State does not allow foreclosure or the appointment of a Receiver.

And both LLCs can just retain the distributions, but send the Schedule K-1 to the holder of the Judgment Lien so that he can pay the taxes.

The Nevada LLC owns the LLC that owns the real estate. You own the Nevada LLC. The Nevada law on Charging Orders protects your Capital Interest if you are sued.

SINGLE MEMBER AND MULTI MEMBER

A Limited Partnership (LP) will always have more than a single member. It will have a General Partner and one or more Limited Partners.

But an LLC can be either a Single Member LLC, called a SMLLC, or a Multi Member LLC, called a MMLLC.

And in addition to the States with weak Charging Order protections, there is another problem with some other States.

Some States do not provide the same Charging Order protection to SMLLCs that they offer to MMLLCs.

Charging Order protection is denied completely to SMLLCs in:

1.) California,

2.) Colorado,

3.) Georgia,

4.) Florida,

5.) Kansas, and

6.) New York.

On the other hand, States with statutes that clearly say that the Charging Order is the only remedy available to the holder of the Judgment Lien are:

1.) Nevada,

2.) Wyoming,

3.) Delaware,

4.) South Dakota, and

5.) Alaska.

The statutes and the court cases of the remaining States fall somewhere in between these two extremes.

It is not true that Nevada and Wyoming have allowed bypassing the Charging Order protection for SMLLCs.

The two cases cited in the books by authors hawking their services and claiming to be knowledgeable about this, were not based on the LLCs having single members instead of multiple members.

The two cases involved a Bankruptcy in one case, and a case of piercing the corporate veil due to blatant undercapitalization and irresponsible manipulative management in the other.

The verdicts would have been the same if the entities had been MMLLCs.

So you might want to laugh off the invitation to pay their "affiliated agency" over a thousand dollars to show you how to gift 5% of your LLC to your child through the Uniform Gift To Minors Act, or set up a Revocable Trust, which is not even a legal entity, so that you will not be a SMLLC.

CONCLUSION

The Limited Liability Company (LLC) is getting old enough to have some solid case law to explain it and back it up. And the true social and political attitudes of the various States are becoming pretty well established.

It looks like there will be 15 or 20 States that will not be friendly to the LLC form of business.

But it looks like there will be an equal number where the LLC will exist as it was originally intended, as a reasonable limit of liability for businessmen willing to incur the expenses and risk the uncertainty of operating a business.

Right now, there are about five strong LLC environments.

1.) Nevada,

2.) Wyoming,

3.) Delaware,

4.) South Dakota, and

5.) Alaska.

In the past couple of years, at least three other States have amended their LLC statutes to almost copy the Delaware statutes.

And two of those State are pushing to establish the types of Business Courts that Delaware has, where business cases are heard by Judges who actually know what is going on, instead of Judges that hear divorces, criminal, juvenile, and everything else.

The friendly business environments in Delaware and Nevada are providing huge amounts of revenue for those State governments, and some of the other States are paying close attention.

Nevada, South Dakota, Alaska, and Wyoming also have the advantage of no State income tax.

If you live in one of the weak States, you just have to deal with the situation, and decide how much risk you are willing to tolerate.

You might just want to use a separate LLC for each of your rental properties, and keep the loans as high as you can, so that there is as little equity as possible.

Or you might want to go ahead and operate with a Delaware or Nevada LLC and have it own the other LLC which are holding the real estate.

But you need to understand the situation, and make your decision.

YOUR BEST BUSINESS ENTITY

MICHAEL LANTRIP

Made in the USA
San Bernardino, CA
06 November 2019